YOUR recipe could appear in our next cookbook!

Share your tried & true family favorites with us instantly at

www.gooseberrypatch.com

If you'd rather jot 'em down by hand, just mail this form to...

Gooseberry Patch • Cookbooks – Call for Recipes
PO Box 812 • Columbus, OH 43216-0812

If your recipe is selected for a book, you'll receive a FREE copy!

Please share only your original recipes or those that you have made your own over the years.

Recipe Name:

Number of Servings:

Any fond memories about this recipe? Special touches you like to add
or handy shortcuts?

Ingredients (include specific measurements):

Instructions (continue on back if needed):

Special Code: **cookbookspage**

Over ➤

Extra space for recipe if needed:

Tell us about yourself...

Your complete contact information is needed so that we can send you your FREE cookbook, if your recipe is published. Phone numbers and email addresses are kept private and will only be used if we have questions about your recipe.

Name:

Address:

City: State: Zip:

Email:

Daytime Phone:

Thank you! Vickie & Jo Ann

Christmas
at Grandma's

Gooseberry Patch

An imprint of Globe Pequot
246 Goose Lane
Guilford, CT 06437

www.gooseberrypatch.com
1•800•854•6673

Copyright 2014, Gooseberry Patch   978-1-62093-173-8

Do you have a tried & true recipe...

tip, craft or memory that you'd like to see featured in
a **Gooseberry Patch** cookbook? Visit our website at
www.gooseberrypatch.com, register and follow the
easy steps to submit your favorite family recipe.
Or send them to us at:

Gooseberry Patch
PO Box 812
Columbus, OH 43216-0812

Don't forget to include the number of servings your recipe makes,
plus your name, address, phone number and email address. If we
select your recipe, your name will appear right along with it...
and you'll receive a **FREE** copy of the book!

Contents

Dedication

To every busy mom who wants to share an old-fashioned Christmas with her family.

Appreciation

To Grandma, Gram, Granny, Mimi and Nonna...thanks for all the recipes, memories and love!

Waking up
at Grandma's

Buttermilk Coffee Cake

Cheryl Gray
Warrenton, MO

Recently I came across my mom's handwritten recipe for coffee cake. Sometimes, if we had a snow day from school, Mom would make it for my brother and me. Its wonderful aroma filled the house. Now I make it for my husband and me, and when I go home to visit my dad, I always make a couple to freeze and take to him. It is one of the few recipes I can make that taste just like Mom used to make.

1 c. raisins	1/2 c. shortening
2 c. boiling water	1/2 t. salt
4 c. all-purpose flour	2 t. baking soda
2 c. sugar	2 c. buttermilk
1-1/2 t. cinnamon	

Combine raisins and boiling water. Let stand for 10 minutes; drain. In a large bowl, mix together flour, sugar and cinnamon; cut in shortening with a fork. Set aside 1/3 cup of mixture for topping. Add salt, baking soda, buttermilk and raisins. Mix well; batter will be thick. Divide batter evenly between 2 greased and floured 9" round cake pans. Sprinkle reserved topping over batter. Bake at 375 degrees for 35 minutes, or until cake tests done with a toothpick inserted in the center. Cool for about 10 minutes; remove from pan. Serve immediately, or wrap in aluminum foil. May be frozen. To serve, cut into slices. Makes 2 coffee cakes, 6 to 8 servings per cake.

Have a breakfast get-together for friends & neighbors. Serve coffee cake, juices and fruit before a busy day of holiday shopping and decorating...how neighborly!

GG's Pancake Sausage Breakfast
Julie Dossantos
Fort Pierce, FL

This recipe is directly from my Grandma "GG." It brings back many wonderful childhood memories of family Christmases spent at my grandparents' home in Arkansas.

10 to 12 brown & serve
   breakfast sausages
2 c. pancake mix

1 c. milk
3 eggs, beaten
Garnish: maple syrup

Brown sausages according to package directions; drain on a paper towel-lined plate. In a bowl, combine pancake mix, milk and eggs. Blend well. Pour batter into a greased 13"x9" baking pan. Arrange sausages in rows across the batter. Sausages will sink to the bottom. Bake at 350 degrees for 30 minutes, or until a toothpick tests clean. Cut into servings, allowing one sausage per serving. Serve with syrup. Makes 10 to 12 servings.

A Christmas wreath for breakfast! Simply arrange refrigerated cinnamon rolls on a baking sheet in a wreath shape and bake as usual. Frost and decorate with candied cherries.

Biscuits & Gravy Casserole

Audra Vanhorn-Sorey
Columbia, NC

When I was growing up in a country home, my mother always made homemade biscuits and sawmill gravy on Christmas morning. This recipe tastes homemade, in half the time!

1/2 lb. ground pork breakfast
   sausage
3 T. all-purpose flour
2-1/2 c. whole milk

1/2 t. salt
1/2 t. pepper
16-oz. tube refrigerated jumbo
   flaky biscuits

In a heavy skillet, cook sausage over medium heat until browned; do not drain. Sprinkle flour over sausage in pan; stir well. Add milk, salt and pepper; stir to combine. Cook, stirring frequently, just until mixture comes to a boil. If gravy is too thick, stir in a little more milk to desired consistency. Pour gravy into an 11"x7" baking pan coated with non-stick vegetable spray. Arrange unbaked biscuits over gravy. Bake at 400 degrees for 25 minutes, or until biscuits are golden. Serves 6 to 8.

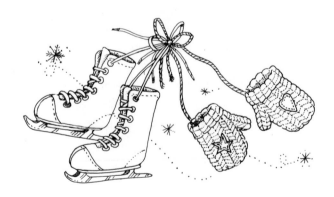

A cheerful greeting for visitors...hang a pair of ice skates
and a pair of woolly mittens on the front door
with a big bow.

Christmas Sausage Soufflé

Carol Jordan
Gilbert, AZ

I got the basis for this recipe from my sister in Utah and have been making it for my family ever since. That was over 20 years ago! On Christmas morning, I put this in to bake and then we enjoy our time opening presents with the wonderful smell of baking breakfast.

10 eggs, beaten
1-1/2 c. plus 2/3 c. milk,
 divided
salt and pepper to taste
2 c. ground pork breakfast
 sausage, browned and
 drained

20 slices white bread, torn into
 small pieces
2-1/2 c. shredded Cheddar
 cheese
10-3/4 oz. can cream of
 mushroom soup

In a large bowl, whisk together eggs, 1-1/2 cups milk, salt and pepper. Stir in sausage, bread and cheese. Cover and refrigerate overnight. In the morning, transfer mixture to a greased 13"x9" baking pan. In a separate bowl, whisk together soup and remaining milk; spoon over top. Bake, uncovered, at 350 degrees for 1-1/2 hours, or until set. Makes 15 servings.

When I was a child, my family gathered at my grandma's house on Christmas. There would be the wonderful smell of ham baking, tons of family and Grandma in a Christmas sweater! All the kids would load up in her van and drive around town looking at Christmas lights and singing Christmas carols. When we returned, the Christmas tree was no longer bare...Santa had come while we were gone! It was magical to us children. My grandma is no longer with us, but she left a special feeling in my heart around the holidays.

–Gretchen Raines, South Charleston, OH

Raspberry Breakfast Rolls

Andrea Heyart
Savannah, TX

*Blueberry, blackberry, and strawberry all work great in these rolls...
use your favorite flavor or do half & half with two flavors. Variety
makes it easy to feed a house full of holiday house guests!*

3/4 c. seedless raspberry jam
1/4 c. butter, softened
1/2 t. cinnamon

2 8-oz. tubes refrigerated
   crescent roll dough sheets

In a bowl, stir together jam, butter and cinnamon. Unroll crescent roll
sheets; spread jam mixture evenly over each. Roll up each sheet
tightly starting on one long edge. With a knife or plain dental floss,
cut each roll into 8 to 10 equal slices. Arrange cut-side up in a greased
13"x9" baking pan or two 9" round cake pans. Bake at 375 degrees
for 20 to 25 minutes, until golden. Let cool for 5 to 10 minutes;
spread with Frosting. Makes 16 to 20 servings.

Frosting:

3-oz. pkg. cream cheese,
  softened
1/2 c. butter, softened
3 c. powdered sugar

1 t. vanilla extract
1 T. seedless raspberry jam
2 to 3 T. milk, divided

In a bowl, blend together cream cheese and butter. Stir in powdered
sugar, vanilla, jam and one tablespoon milk. If too thick, stir in
remaining milk, one tablespoon at a time, to desired consistency.

Aprons are practical, but also adorable! Look for the 1950s style
with poinsettias, snowmen and Santa Claus...perfect gifts for
girlfriends who love to cook.

Cinnamon Roll Cherry Cobbler *Carrie Kelderman*
Pella, IA

We tweaked this cobbler from my grandmother's recipe. Our kids love it, and it makes a very special breakfast surprise on Christmas!

21-oz. can cherry pie filling
3 T. red cinnamon candies
12-oz. tube refrigerated
   cinnamon rolls

1/2 c. powdered sugar
1 T. lemon juice

In a saucepan over medium heat, combine pie filling and candies. Cook and stir until bubbly. Spoon mixture into a greased 8"x8" baking pan. Arrange cinnamon rolls on top, setting aside frosting packet for another use. Bake at 400 degrees for 20 minutes, or until golden. For glaze, stir together powdered sugar and lemon juice until smooth; drizzle over cobbler. Serve warm, cut into squares. Serves 4 to 6.

Help the kids mix up some "Magic Reindeer Food" just for fun! Fill a plastic sandwich bag with a big spoonful of uncooked oats, a dash of sugar and some candy sprinkles. On Christmas Eve they can sprinkle it on the lawn to guide Santa's reindeer to your home.

Egg & Cheese Holiday Pie

Alice Zecco
Socorro, NM

A family tradition! We only have this twice a year, Thanksgiving and Christmas mornings. It started with a recipe from a friend's child for breakfast pizza, and just evolved into a pie. It's a great make-ahead. Try it with bacon too...precooked bacon cuts down on prep time. There are usually no leftovers!

1 to 2 lbs. ground pork
    breakfast sausage
2 potatoes, peeled and grated
1 onion, chopped
4 slices American cheese,
    chopped and divided
1 c. shredded Cheddar cheese,
    divided

1 c. shredded mozzarella cheese,
    divided
2 9-inch deep-dish pie crusts
1 doz. eggs
1/4 c. milk

Brown sausage in a large skillet over medium heat; drain. Divide potatoes, onion, sausage and half of the cheeses between unbaked pie crusts, layering evenly. In a large bowl, whisk eggs with milk. Pour evenly into crusts, filling no more than 3/4 full. Top pies with remaining cheeses. Bake at 350 degrees for 45 to 60 minutes, until a knife tip inserted into centers comes out clean. Cool slightly; cut into wedges. May also bake, then refrigerate overnight and reheat in the microwave. Makes 2 pies; each serves 6 to 8.

Add whimsy to the breakfast table! Bring your grandmother's old salt & pepper shakers out of the cupboard...use an old cow-shaped pitcher to serve up milk for cereal.

Pineapple Coffee Cake

Bridget Jenkinson
Greenville, OH

*When hosting a crowd for breakfast I like to serve
this delicious coffee cake. It's always a hit!*

1 c. sugar
1 c. canola oil
1 t. vanilla extract
4 eggs

2 c. all-purpose flour
1 t. baking powder
21-oz. can pineapple pie filling

In a bowl, beat sugar, oil and vanilla by hand until blended. Beat in eggs, one at a time. Add flour and baking powder; mix well. Pour half of batter into a greased 13"x9" baking pan. Spoon pie filling over batter; pour remaining batter over pie filling. Swirl top layer of batter with a knife. Bake at 375 degrees for 45 to 50 minutes, until center tests done with a toothpick. Let cool in pan on a wire rack. Drizzle with Powdered Sugar Glaze; cut into squares. Makes 12 to 15 servings.

Powdered Sugar Glaze:

1 c. powdered sugar
1/2 t. vanilla extract

2 T. milk or water

Combine powdered sugar, vanilla and enough milk or water for a drizzling consistency.

Tuck a packet of spiced tea into a Christmas card to
a dear friend...she can enjoy a hot cup of tea while
enjoying your greeting.

Mrs. Glaser's Williamsburg Soufflé

Sandra Smith
Quartz Hill, CA

My husband was the best man for his best friend's wedding. The day before the wedding, the bride's mother made a wonderful brunch. I fell in love with this dish and asked her for the recipe. I have been making it ever since, and that was over 20 years ago!

8 slices day-old egg bread	2 T. all-purpose flour
1/4 c. butter	8 eggs, beaten
2 c. sliced mushrooms	2 c. half-and-half
1 c. onion, minced	2 T. mustard
2 c. cooked ham, diced	1 T. garlic salt
16-oz. pkg. shredded Cheddar cheese	1 t. salt

Trim crusts from bread; cut bread into bite-size cubes. Arrange bread cubes in a greased 13"x9" baking pan; set aside. Melt butter in a skillet over medium heat; sauté mushrooms and onion for about 5 minutes. Spoon mixture evenly over bread cubes; top with ham. In a large bowl, sprinkle cheese with flour; toss well and spread over ham layer. In a separate bowl, whisk eggs with half-and-half, mustard and salts. Pour over cheese layer. Cover and refrigerate overnight. Uncover; bake at 325 degrees for one hour, or until puffy and lightly golden. Serves 8 to 10.

Tie tiny Christmas ornaments onto stemmed glasses with ribbon bows...so festive at a holiday brunch.

14

Waking up at Grandma's

Mom's Cheese Grits

Elizabeth Smithson
Cunningham, KY

Mom always served us this recipe for special breakfasts! It's been in the family for years, from her mom on down. Now I serve it for brunch with my church ladies...they always ask for the recipe.

2 eggs, beaten
1/4 to 1/2 c. milk
1 c. long-cooking grits,
   uncooked

1 t. garlic, minced
1/2 c. butter, sliced
2 c. shredded Cheddar cheese,
   divided

Combine eggs with enough milk to equal one cup; set aside. Cook grits according to package directions; remove from heat. Add garlic, butter and one cup cheese; stir until butter and cheese melt. Stir in egg mixture. Pour into a greased 2-quart casserole dish; sprinkle with remaining cheese. Bake, uncovered, at 350 degrees for 20 minutes. Serves 7 to 8.

Oven-Baked Home Fries

Krista Marshall
Fort Wayne, IN

Nothing goes better with a big breakfast than homemade home fries! These are so simple to prepare and the oven does the work for you.

5 to 6 redskin potatoes, cut into
   1-inch cubes
1/4 c. oil
2 t. seasoned salt

2 t. paprika
1 t. dried parsley
pepper to taste

In an ungreased 11"x7" baking pan, combine potatoes and oil. Sprinkle with seasonings; toss to coat well. Bake, uncovered, at 400 degrees for one hour, or until potatoes are tender and golden, stirring halfway through. Serves 4 to 6.

For the fluffiest scrambled eggs ever, try Grandma's secret...
stir in a pinch of baking powder.

Farmers' Breakfast Casserole

Liz Brooks
Lexington, KY

My husband grew up on a farm and he loves this hearty casserole.
The hot sauce really makes this dish tasty, so don't leave it out! It
doesn't make it hot, just pumps up the flavors.

3 c. frozen shredded
  hashbrowns
2 c. cooked ham, cubed
1 bunch green onions, chopped
4 eggs, beaten
12-oz. can evaporated milk

1 T. hot pepper sauce
1 t. smoked paprika
1 t. pepper
1-1/2 c. shredded sharp
  Cheddar cheese

Spread frozen hashbrowns in an 8"x8" glass baking pan sprayed with
non-stick vegetable spray. Sprinkle ham and onions over hashbrowns.
In a bowl, whisk together eggs, evaporated milk, hot sauce and
seasonings. Pour over ham layer; top with cheese. Bake, uncovered,
at 375 degrees for 55 to 60 minutes, until hot and cheese is golden.
Slice into squares; serve immediately. If making a double recipe, use a
13"x9" baking pan and increase baking time by 10 to 15 minutes.
Makes 4 to 6 servings.

A sweet keepsake for a family brunch. Copy one of Grandma's
tried & true recipes onto a festive card, then punch a hole
in the corner and tie the card to a rolled napkin with
a length of ribbon.

B's Cornbread Sausage Bites

Bren Rogers
Atwood, CA

These tasty little morsels are sure to be as big a favorite in your home on Christmas morning as they are in ours. Easy, yummy and can be eaten on the go too.

6 brown & serve breakfast
   sausages
8-1/2 oz. pkg. corn muffin mix

Optional: 1/2 c. shredded
   Cheddar cheese

Brown sausages according to package directions. Drain on a paper towel-lined plate; cut each sausage in half. Meanwhile, prepare corn muffin mix according to package directions. Spoon batter into 12 paper-lined mini muffin cups. Place one piece of sausage into the center of each muffin. Sprinkle with cheese, if desired. Bake muffins at 400 degrees for 15 to 20 minutes, just until golden. Cool before serving. Makes one dozen.

Uncles and aunts, and cousins, are all very well,
and fathers and mothers are not to be despised; but a
grandmother, at holiday time, is worth them all.

–Fanny Fern

Miss Rosetta's Cherry Almond Scones

Pearl Rosetta Teiserskas
Brookfield, IL

My grandmother was a wonderful southern cook, born and raised in Key West, Florida. She got up early in the morning to bake these wonderful scones for us. We could smell the aroma from the second-floor loft where we slept three to a bed. Share with friends!

1/2 c. sliced almonds
1/2 c. plus 2 T. sugar, divided
1/8 t. nutmeg
2-1/2 c. all-purpose flour
2 t. baking powder
1/2 t. salt

1/2 c. butter, softened
3/4 c. sour cream
1 egg, beaten
1/2 t. almond extract
2/3 c. sweetened dried cherries,
    coarsely chopped

Combine almonds, 2 tablespoons sugar and nutmeg in a small bowl. Mix well and set aside. In a large bowl, stir together flour, remaining sugar, baking powder and salt. Add butter; mix with a fork or pastry blender until mixture resembles coarse crumbs. In a separate bowl, combine sour cream, egg and extract; stir until well mixed. Add sour cream mixture to flour mixture; mix until moistened. Fold in cherries. Turn dough onto a lightly floured surface. Knead 6 to 8 times, until smooth; add a small amount of flour if needed. Divide dough in half; pat each half into a 7-inch circle on a lightly greased baking sheet. Sprinkle almond mixture evenly over circles. Lightly score each circle into 8 wedges; do not cut apart. Bake at 375 degrees for 25 to 30 minutes, until lightly golden. Cool for 10 minutes; separate wedges. Makes 16 scones.

Dress up homemade scones in a snap...drizzle with melted white chocolate or powdered sugar icing.

Ginger Ale Biscuits

Marsha Joiner
Woodbridge, VA

I used to make my Grandmother Parker's biscuits from her scratch recipe, which was a bit of this & a pinch of that. But this recipe is so simple and good, I admit to taking an easier way out...sorry, Grandma!.

1/4 c. butter, melted
2 c. biscuit baking mix

1/2 c. sour cream
1/2 c. ginger ale

Spread melted butter in a 9"x9" baking pan; set aside. Combine remaining ingredients in a bowl. Whisk until a sticky dough forms. Drop dough into pan by tablespoonfuls, making rows of 3 until all dough is used. Spoonfuls of dough will be touching. Bake at 400 degrees for about 12 minutes, until golden. Serves 4 to 6.

Mimie's Chocolate Gravy

Beckie Apple
Grannis, AR

My brother and I loved to spend the weekend with my Grandmother Mimie and Pop for many reasons, including her wonderfully rich and delicious chocolate gravy with hot buttered biscuits for breakfast.

2-1/2 T. baking cocoa
3/4 c. sugar
3 T. all-purpose flour
1/4 t. salt

2 c. milk
2 T. butter, sliced
1 t. vanilla extract
hot biscuits, split

In a bowl, mix cocoa, sugar, flour and salt; set aside. In a saucepan over medium-low heat, bring milk, butter and vanilla to a low boil. Quickly whisk cocoa mixture into hot milk mixture. Continue whisking until well blended; cook and stir until thickened. Immediately remove from heat. Serve over biscuits. Serves 6.

Set out peppermint sticks for stirring breakfast cocoa...it's Christmas!

Grampa's Sunday Waffles

Steve Tatham
Plymouth, NH

These waffles are a must on Sunday mornings whenever our granddaughters are here for the weekend! They're best served with Grammy's Homemade "Maple" Syrup. It's not maple syrup at all, just a simple brown sugar syrup, but the girls love it.

2 eggs	2-1/2 c. all-purpose flour
2-1/4 c. milk	1-1/2 T. sugar
1/2 c. butter, melted and slightly cooled	4 t. baking powder
1 t. vanilla extract	3/4 t. salt

In a large bowl, beat eggs with an electric mixer on low speed. Beat in milk, butter and vanilla. In a separate bowl, combine remaining ingredients and mix well. Add to egg mixture; beat until smooth. Add batter to a heated greased waffle iron by rounded 1/4 cupfuls. Cook until golden, according to manufacturer's directions. Serve with Grammy's Homemade "Maple" Syrup. Leftover waffles will reheat well in the microwave. Makes 10 to 12 waffles.

Grammy's Homemade "Maple" Syrup:

1 c. water	2 c. brown sugar

In a saucepan over medium-high heat, combine ingredients. Bring to a boil; reduce heat and simmer 5 minutes. Serve warm or cool. Refrigerate any leftover syrup in a covered jar.

Ho-Ho-Ho! Invite a local Santa to drop in during this year's family get-together. What a joy for all ages!

Christmas Eve French Toast

Jill Ball
Highland, UT

Our family looks forward to Christmas Eve all year. We pack the day with fun family traditions, one of which is this delicious breakfast. We like to top ours with cranberry jam.

12 slices firm, dry cinnamon
   raisin bread
2 c. dairy eggnog

1/2 c. butter
Garnish: powdered sugar

Trim crusts from bread; cut bread into 1-inch strips. Pour eggnog into a shallow bowl. Dip each strip of bread into eggnog, coating well on both sides. Melt butter in a skillet over medium heat. Add bread strips; cook bread on both sides until golden. Dust with powdered sugar. Makes 12 servings.

I'll never forget the Christmas back in the 1950s when my sister and I received the best gifts of our childhood. We had asked Santa for every little girl's dream doll, called a "three-year-old doll." As we ran excitedly down the stairs on Christmas morning, we immediately spotted our requested dolls along with two neatly folded stacks of fabric and handwritten notes from "Mrs. Claus" sitting on top. She wrote to explain that this had been a very busy year, and apologized for not having had time to make outfits for our new dolls. Mrs. Santa said that if we continued to be very good little girls, she was sure our mother would be glad to make them for us. While we loved our dolls, the notes from Mrs. Claus were by far the most treasured and best gifts we ever received.

–Pat Beach, Fisherville, KY

Christmas Morning Egg Skillet

Cinda Lasinski
Centennial, CO

When my sons Richard and David were young, their grandma started an annual Christmas brunch tradition and served this egg casserole. We've continued her tradition ourselves, even after our sons married and had kids of their own years later. Mom passed away in 2010, but she is fondly remembered when we serve her delicious breakfast dish.

1/2 c. onion, chopped
1 to 2 t. olive oil
1-1/2 doz. eggs
1 to 2 c. ground pork breakfast sausage, browned, or cooked ham, cubed

6-oz. pkg. turkey or chicken-flavored stuffing mix, prepared
1 to 2 c. shredded mozzarella or Cheddar cheese

In a small skillet over medium heat, sauté onion in olive oil. Whisk eggs in a large bowl; stir in onion mixture, sausage or ham and stuffing. Spray a large skillet with non-stick vegetable spray. Pour egg mixture into skillet, working in batches if necessary. Cook over medium-low heat, stirring constantly, until eggs are set. Stir in desired amount of cheese; let stand several minutes, until melted. Makes 10 to 12 servings.

Decorate the kitchen for the holidays! Tie cheery bows on cabinet knobs, hang cookie cutters in the window and tuck sprigs of fresh pine into sifters, mixing bowls and canisters.

Country Potato Cakes

Carly St. Clair
Lynnwood, WA

My grandmother used to make these with leftover mashed potatoes and they were so delicious. Her secret was a well seasoned cast-iron skillet which gives a nice flavor and aids in even browning. Great with meals any time of day!

2 eggs, beaten
1/2 t. salt
1/4 t. pepper
3 c. mashed potatoes
1/2 c. all-purpose flour

1/2 c. green onions, diced
1/2 c. shredded Cheddar Jack
 cheese
canola oil for frying

In a bowl, whisk eggs with salt and pepper. Stir in remaining ingredients except oil; set aside. Meanwhile, add one inch oil to a cast-iron skillet over medium-high heat. Heat until oil is very hot but not smoking, about 375 degrees. Add potato mixture to oil by 1/2 cupfuls. Cook until golden on the bottom. With a spatula, turn potato cakes over and flatten. Cook until golden on other side. Drain on paper towels; serve hot. Makes 6 to 8 servings.

Warm breakfast casseroles and freshly baked coffee cakes travel well in insulated containers...perfect for a snowy picnic after cutting down the Christmas tree. Add a thermos of hot cocoa. Memories in the making!

Grandma's Caramel Apple Bake

Teresa Eller
Tonganoxie, KS

A scrumptious brunch dish your guests will love. It's so convenient since you make it ahead of time, then refrigerate.

1 loaf French bread, cubed
   and divided
2 egg whites, beaten
1 c. brown sugar, packed
2 apples, peeled, cored
   and chopped

1 T. cinnamon
8 eggs, beaten
1/2 c. milk
1/2 t. vanilla extract
1/2 t. almond extract
Garnish: chopped pecans

Place half of bread in a 13"x9" baking pan sprayed with non-stick vegetable spray. In a bowl, stir together egg whites, brown sugar, apples and cinnamon. Spoon mixture over bread in pan; add remaining bread. In a separate bowl, whisk together eggs, milk and extracts. Pour over bread; press mixture down with your hands. Cover with aluminum foil; refrigerate for 8 hours to overnight. In the morning, place pan in a cold oven; turn on oven to 350 degrees. Bake for 40 to 45 minutes, until golden. Serve portions topped with Caramel Topping and pecans. Serves 8 to 10.

Caramel Topping :

1/2 c. butter, sliced
1 c. brown sugar, packed

1/4 c. milk

Combine all ingredients in a saucepan over medium heat. Bring to a boil. Boil for 3 minutes, stirring often. Remove from heat; cool slightly.

Make a memory with a little one by creating a simple paper chain... decorate the tree or count down to the big day with each loop!

Waking up at Grandma's

Jordan Marsh Blueberry Muffins

Julie Dobson
Richmond Hill, GA

When we were kids, my mom used to take my sister and me shopping at Jordan Marsh department store in Boston. We always stopped by their bakery to get a blueberry muffin. Mom got the recipe and we've made them ever since. Although the store no longer exists, we can still enjoy these wonderful muffins.

1/2 c. butter, softened
1 c. plus 2 t. sugar, divided
2 eggs
2 c. all-purpose flour
2 t. baking powder

1/2 t. salt
1/2 c. milk
1 t. vanilla extract
2-1/2 c. fresh or frozen
   blueberries

Combine butter and one cup sugar in a large bowl; beat with an electric mixer on medium speed until fluffy. Add eggs and beat again; set aside. In a separate bowl, sift together flour, remaining sugar, baking powder and salt. Add flour mixture to butter mixture alternately with milk and vanilla; beat until moistened. Stir in blueberries by hand. Fill greased muffin cups 2/3 full. Bake at 375 degrees for 25 to 30 minutes, until a toothpick tests clean. Cool muffins in tin for 30 minutes; remove to a wire rack. Makes one dozen.

Baking together is a fun family activity and a great choice for kids just starting to learn how to cook. As you measure and mix together, be sure to share any stories about hand-me-down recipes...you'll be creating memories as well as sweet treats!

Sleep-Over Cinnamon Toast

Cyndy DeStefano
Mercer, PA

My daughter Rachel often has sleepovers with several of her friends. Cinnamon toast is a favorite and this is an easy way to make enough all at once. I serve this with fruit juice in fancy glasses...perfect for a bunch of giggly kids!

1/2 c. butter, softened
1/2 c. sugar
1 t. cinnamon

1 t. vanilla extract
8 slices white bread

In a bowl, mash butter with a fork. Stir in other ingredients except bread until well mixed. Spread butter mixture generously on one side of each slice of bread. Arrange bread on an ungreased baking sheet, butter-side up. Bake at 350 degrees for 10 minutes. Turn on broiler; broil until topping is bubbly. Serves 4.

Whip up some good old-fashioned snow ice cream. Beat one cup heavy cream until soft peaks form, then fold in four cups freshly fallen snow. Add sugar and vanilla to taste. A wonderful wintertime treat!

Christmas Dreams Cocoa Mix
Elizabeth Cassinos
Paradise Valley, NV

Many years ago I bought a delicious cocoa mix at a craft festival. Once I ran out I couldn't get any more, so I recreated this spicy cocoa treat...it tastes like Christmas in a cup!

1 c. chocolate drink mix	1 T. finely ground nutmeg
1/4 c. powdered sugar	2 t. cinnamon

Mix all ingredients together and store in an airtight container, or package in small jars for gifts. Attach directions. Makes 10 to 12 servings.

Directions:

To 2/3 cup hot water, add one heaping tablespoon mix, or to taste. Stir well.

Scoop Christmas Dreams Cocoa Mix into plastic icing cones and fill any extra space at the top with mini marshmallows...what a fun gift for co-workers!

Ranchero Breakfast Casserole

Kristi Adducci
Arvada, CO

I put together this dish one snow-day morning when I was working from home. The recipe has been passed on to friends and they tell me I should share it...so, here it is for all to enjoy!

16-oz. pkg. ground pork
  breakfast sausage
6 eggs, beaten
2 c. frozen diced potatoes
10-oz. can diced tomatoes with
  green chiles

10-3/4 oz. can cream of chicken
  soup
pepper and chili powder to taste
1 c. shredded Colby Jack cheese
Garnish: sour cream

In a skillet over medium heat, cook sausage until browned. Set aside sausage; partially drain drippings in skillet. Add eggs to skillet; scramble to desired doneness. Meanwhile, place potatoes in a microwave-safe bowl; microwave until softened. In a large bowl, combine sausage, eggs, potatoes, tomatoes and soup. Add seasonings to taste. Spoon into a greased 11"x7" baking pan; top with cheese. Bake, uncovered, at 350 degrees for 30 to 45 minutes, until bubbly and lightly golden. Garnish with a dollop of sour cream. Makes 4 to 6 servings.

Show off three or four of your most treasured Christmas ornaments...hang them on a countertop coffee mug holder. Finish with a few twists of tinsel.

Spinach & Mushroom Pie

Angela Bissette
Zebulon, NC

I created this delicious recipe one day after tasting something similar in a local restaurant. It is perfect for breakfast, lunch or dinner.

1/2 c. onion, diced
8-oz. jar sliced mushrooms,
   drained
2 cloves garlic, minced
2 T. butter
10-oz. pkg. frozen spinach,
   thawed and drained

9-inch pie crust
3 eggs, beaten
1/2 c. milk
1 c. shredded Cheddar cheese

In a skillet over medium heat, sauté onion, mushrooms and garlic in butter. Add spinach; heat through. Pour onion mixture into unbaked pie crust. In a bowl, whisk together eggs, milk and cheese; pour egg mixture into pie crust. Bake at 350 degrees for 30 to 45 minutes, until set and golden. Cut into wedges. Serves 8.

Tote along a vintage thermos filled with hot cocoa on a visit to the Christmas tree farm...it'll really hit the spot! Before ladling in the cocoa, prewarm the thermos with hot water for 10 minutes.

Mini Dutch Babies

Annette Ingram
Grand Rapids, MI

My grandma used to make an easy oven pancake with the funny name of Dutch Baby, so I was excited to try this mini version. It's a great way to make tender pancakes for everyone at once.

1/2 c. all-purpose flour	2 t. vanilla extract
1/2 c. milk	1/4 t. salt
3 eggs	Garnish: powdered sugar, jam
2 T. sugar	or pancake syrup

Combine all ingredients except garnish in a blender; process on medium speed until smooth. Pour batter into 12 greased muffin cups. Bake at 400 degrees for 13 to 16 minutes, until edges are golden. Cool in tin on a wire rack for 2 minutes; turn out of tin. Dust pancakes with powdered sugar; serve with jam or syrup. Makes 6 servings, 2 pancakes each.

I remember sledding at my grandma's house in Michigan. She had lots of long steep hills and there was always plenty of snow. We would sled until we were on the verge of getting frostbite through our soaked clothing, and then we would come inside to a warm kitchen. Grandma would have hot chocolate and a bag of marshmallows ready for us. My cousins and I would dump in marshmallows until we couldn't fit any more in the cup. Then we would stir our hot chocolate and watch the marshmallows slowly melt while we started to warm up again. We had the most interesting conversations over our cups of hot chocolate! We knew we were well-loved.

–Melissa Ade, Carlton, KS

Homemade Orange Syrup

Brenda Schlosser
Brighton, CO

I first tried this incredible syrup on French toast at an inn in Napa, California. The innkeeper was nice enough to share her recipe. Great on pancakes and waffles, even pound cake. Yum!

6-oz. can frozen orange juice
  concentrate
3 c. brown sugar, packed
1 c. honey

1 lb. butter, sliced
zest of 2 to 3 oranges
Optional: 2 T. maple flavoring

In a large saucepan over medium heat, combine orange juice concentrate, brown sugar and honey. Cook and stir until sugar dissolves; remove from heat. In a separate saucepan over low heat, melt butter with zest and flavoring, if desired. Add butter mixture to orange juice mixture; stir well. Simmer over low heat for 5 minutes, stirring until smooth. Pour into jars; cover and refrigerate up to 2 weeks. Makes 2 quarts.

Santa's Cranberry Waffle Sauce

Sandy Ward
Anderson, IN

This festive sauce is wonderful over pecan waffles...pancakes too.

14-oz. can jellied cranberry
  sauce, sliced

1/4 c. butter, sliced
1/4 c. brown sugar, packed

In a saucepan over medium heat, combine all ingredients. Bring to a boil; stir until smooth and brown sugar is dissolved. Serve warm. Cover and refrigerate any leftovers. Serves 5 to 6.

A vintage canning jar filled with a favorite homemade sauce makes a thoughtful hostess gift. Tie on a topper of colorful holiday fabric with ribbon.

Overnight Sticky Buns

Sandra Monroe
Preston, MD

Put this together on Christmas Eve, then all you have to do on Christmas morning is pop it in the oven. And so good!

1 c. raisins
3/4 c. chopped pecans
24 to 30 frozen dinner rolls
3-1/2 oz. pkg. cook & serve
  butterscotch pudding mix

1/2 c. brown sugar, packed
2 t. cinnamon
1/2 c. sugar
2/3 c. butter, melted

Evenly spread raisins and pecans in a 13"x9" baking pan coated with non-stick vegetable spray. Arrange frozen rolls in pan, leaving a little space in between rolls. Combine dry pudding mix with brown sugar; spread over rolls. Combine cinnamon and sugar; sprinkle over top. Drizzle rolls with melted butter. Cover with plastic wrap that has been sprayed with non-stick spray. Set pan in cold oven for 6 hours to overnight. Remove baking pan from oven. Preheat oven to 350 degrees. Remove plastic wrap and return to oven. Bake at 350 degrees for 25 minutes, or until golden. Makes 2 to 2-1/2 dozen.

An oilcloth tablecloth with brightly colored reindeer or snowmen is oh-so cheerful at breakfast...sticky syrup and jam spills are easily wiped off with a damp sponge!

Holiday
Open House

Old-Timey Pimento Cheese Spread
Caroline Timbs
Batesville, AR

This is an old recipe that my granny always made. She just loved pimento cheese and liked to dress it up in all kinds of different ways.

20-oz. container pimento cheese
1 c. pecans, finely chopped
2-1/4 oz. jar dried beef, finely
  chopped

1 bunch green onions, chopped
snack crackers or cut-up
  vegetables

In a bowl, combine all ingredients except crackers or vegetables. Blend well; cover and refrigerate until well chilled. Serve with crackers or vegetables. Serves 8 to 10.

For take-home gifts, fill mini Mason jars with a favorite homemade spread. Tie on a recipe card and a spreader with a bit of ribbon...guests will love it!

Holiday Open House

Ham & Cheese Puffs

Barb Thorsen
Maple Grove, MN

Grandma first made these one Christmas Eve. We went to church, came home and Santa had come by while we were gone...how did he do that? We enjoyed these treats as we had fun opening our gifts.

1/2 c. butter, softened
1-1/2 c. shredded Cheddar
   cheese

1-1/4 c. cooked ham, chopped
1/4 t. Worcestershire sauce
1 c. all-purpose flour

In a bowl, combine butter, cheese, ham and Worcestershire sauce; mix well. Blend in flour, working by hand if necessary. Form into 1/2 to 3/4-inch balls. Place on baking sheets lightly sprayed with non-stick vegetable spray. Bake at 350 degrees for 15 to 18 minutes, until golden. Serve hot. Makes about 3 dozen.

When I was a little girl, my mom, dad, sister and I would go to Mamaw Ruthie's house on Christmas Eve. Her cozy little house was packed full of relatives and she always had yummy treats for us to eat, including her homemade pimento cheese sandwiches! We loved to lie under Mamaw's Christmas tree and look up at the lights. Dad always "forgot" his camera or batteries at home and would have to run back home to get them during our visit. When we got home that night, Santa had magically already come and we got to open our presents right then! Mom and Dad continued this tradition for many years. They loved it just as much as we did.

–Jessica Duncan, Erwin, TN

Aunt Kathie's Awesome Pineapple Cheese Ball

Jennifer Dorward
Jefferson, GA

We first tried this cheese ball many, many moons ago at my Aunt Kathie's house. We don't live near her anymore, but whenever Mom makes it, we think fondly of my aunt and my cousins, and all the good times we've had together.

2 8-oz. pkgs. cream cheese, softened
8-1/2 oz. can crushed pineapple, drained
1/2 green pepper, finely diced
2 T. onion, finely diced
1/2 t. salt
2 c. chopped walnuts, divided
snack crackers, sliced trail bologna or beef stick

In a large bowl, stir cream cheese until smooth. Blend in pineapple, green pepper, onion, salt and one cup walnuts. Shape into a ball; roll ball in remaining walnuts. Cover with plastic wrap and refrigerate overnight. Serve with crackers and sliced trail bologna or beef stick. Makes 12 servings.

For a quick & easy mantel decoration, spell out "Merry Christmas" with vintage alphabet blocks.

English Muffin Hot Appetizers

Shirley Howie
Foxboro, MA

For as long as I can remember, I've served this delicious appetizer on Christmas Eve. It is so easy to make and everyone loves it!

1 c. shredded Cheddar cheese
1/2 c. mayonnaise
4 slices bacon, crisply cooked
   and crumbled

2 green onions, chopped,
   or 1/2 t. onion powder
5 English muffins, split

Combine cheese, mayonnaise, bacon and onions or onion powder in a bowl. Spread mixture on cut side of English muffins; place on an ungreased baking sheet. Bake at 350 degrees for 10 minutes, or until cheese has melted. Serves 5.

Christmas Soda

Bianca Erickson
Hidden Valley Lake, CA

I love making this festive punch with my family every Christmas. It's simple, delicious and the kids enjoy making it too.

46-oz. bottle cranberry juice
   cocktail, chilled
1/2 gal. raspberry sherbet

2 ltrs. lemon-lime soda or
   ginger ale, chilled

Add 1/4 cup cranberry juice to each of 12 to 15 short, wide glasses. Add one scoop (about 1/2 cup) sherbet to each glass. Fill glasses with soda or ginger ale; serve immediately. Serves 12 to 15.

Add pizazz to an appetizer tray...glue tiny Christmas balls onto long toothpicks for serving.

Marvelous Meatballs

Shirl Parsons
Cape Carteret, NC

My grandma used to have lots of company every Christmas Eve.
She always served these scrumptious meatballs.

1 lb. lean ground beef
1/2 c. dry bread crumbs or
   corn flake cereal crumbs
1/2 c. milk
1 t. salt
1 t. pepper

2 c. brown sugar, packed
2 T. all-purpose flour
1/2 c. vinegar
1/4 c. water
2 T. soy sauce
1 T. catsup

In a bowl, combine beef, bread or cereal crumbs, milk, salt and pepper.
Mix well and form into 24 meatballs. Add meatballs to a skillet over
medium-high heat. Brown on all sides; drain. Meanwhile, mix brown
sugar and flour in a saucepan; stir in remaining ingredients. Bring to a
boil over medium-high heat, stirring constantly. Arrange meatballs in
a lightly greased 2-quart casserole dish; spoon brown sugar sauce
over meatballs. Bake, uncovered, at 350 degrees for 20 minutes.
Makes 2 dozen.

Begin a Christmas scrapbook and fill it with copies of
letters to Santa, wish lists and holiday photos...
sweet memories to enjoy in the future.

Holiday Open House

Christmas Cocktail Wieners

Missy Abbott
Hickory, PA

This is so quick & easy! I have been making these little yummies for many years for our annual Christmas party. The recipe has been in our family since I was a little girl...back in those days, it was served as a main dish using full-size wieners. I have also made this recipe with mini smoked sausages with equally delicious results.

2 16-oz. pkgs. cocktail wieners
1 c. brown sugar, packed

1/2 c. catsup
1/4 c. horseradish

Place wieners in a 3-quart slow cooker. Combine remaining ingredients in a bowl; add to wieners and stir gently to coat. Cover and cook on low setting for 4 to 5 hours, or on high setting for 2 to 3 hours. Makes 15 to 20 servings.

Gather friends & family together for a tree-trimming party!
Lay out a simple buffet of finger foods and put Christmas carols
on the stereo...what could be easier or more enjoyable?

GrandMary's Shrimp Spread

Nancy Albers Shore
Cheyenne, WY

My husband's Grandma Mary, GrandMary for short, lives on in our hearts and her recipes. I found this recipe in her recipe box. It is a favorite of all the boys in our family, including my husband and his brother. All the nephews ever request for Christmas dinner is this spread! Feel welcome to substitute light dairy products, but not fat-free versions.

8-oz. pkg. cream cheese, softened
1/4 c. sour cream
2 4-oz. cans cocktail shrimp, drained, or 1 c. cooked shrimp, chopped

1 c. favorite salsa, or to taste
potato or tortilla chips

In a bowl, blend cream cheese and sour cream; stir in shrimp. Add salsa to the desired dipping consistency. Cover and chill for one to 2 hours. Transfer to a serving bowl; serve with chips for dipping. Makes 6 to 8 servings.

An old-fashioned trick to make a taper candle fit snugly in its holder...wrap a rubber band several times around the bottom of the candle. No need to worry about it tipping.

Holiday Crab & Artichoke Dip

Ronda Nading
Rochester, MN

Every Christmas Eve holds dear memories. After church service, we always had a Christmas Eve buffet. We spent most of the day preparing for our feast...everyone pitched in to chop ingredients, put together cookie trays and decorate the table. This dip is served only once a year, so everyone digs right in and enjoys it!

8-oz. pkg. cream cheese,
   room temperature
1 c. mayonnaise
1/3 c. onion, chopped
8-oz. pkg. chunky imitation
   crabmeat, chopped
14-oz. can artichoke hearts,
   drained and chopped

3/4 c. shredded Parmesan
   cheese
1/4 c. grated Romano cheese
1/8 t. nutmeg
snack crackers or sliced French
   bread

In a large bowl, blend cream cheese and mayonnaise until smooth. Stir in remaining ingredients except crackers or bread. Spoon mixture into a lightly greased 9" pie plate. Bake, uncovered, at 425 degrees for 25 minutes, or until lightly golden and heated through. Serve with crackers or bread slices. Makes 12 servings.

Cut out bite-size pieces of fresh red, green and yellow pepper
with a star-shaped mini cookie cutter...what a clever way
to trim a veggie dip platter!

Teriyaki Wing Dings

Jennie Gist
Gooseberry Patch

*This oldie-but-goodie came from a community cookbook over
25 years ago. Recently I ran across it again...be sure to have
plenty of napkins, because it's still finger-lickin' good!*

3 lbs. chicken wings, separated
1/3 c. lemon juice
1/4 c. catsup
1/4 c. soy sauce

1/4 c. oil
2 T. brown sugar, packed
1/4 t. garlic powder
1/4 t. pepper

Place chicken wings in a large plastic zipping bag; set aside. Combine
remaining ingredients in a bowl. Mix well; pour over wings. Seal bag
and refrigerate overnight, turning bag occasionally. Arrange wings
on a wire rack in a greased shallow 15"x10" jelly-roll pan. Bake at
375 degrees for 40 to 45 minutes, turning and basting several times
with pan juices, until golden and chicken juices run clear. Makes 2 to
3 dozen.

When my brother and I were kids, every Christmas Eve we
would go with my parents and Grandma to evening church
service, then back to Grandma's house for our annual Christmas
Eve celebration. Grandma would have a smorgasbord of delicious
cheeses, shrimp cocktails, chicken wings and so many sweets to
devour, all set out on decorative plates. After eating, we opened
gifts around the Christmas tree. Grandma always paid attention
to every detail for decorations, gifts and food! It was a truly
magical night and we looked forward to it every year...our special
time with Grandma. Now that I am grown up, my husband, my
son and I still go to her house on Christmas Eve. My son gets to
experience the same joys that we did when we were young!

–Katie Ventre, Saint Cloud, FL

Holiday Open House

Foolproof Stuffed Mushrooms

Elizabeth Cerri
Stephens City, VA

The secret is in the sherry! I serve these as an appetizer...
they're a favorite.

12 large white mushrooms,
   about 2 inches in diameter
1 shallot, chopped
2 T. butter, sliced
1/4 c. sherry
1/2 c. seasoned dry bread
   crumbs

1/2 c. shredded mozzarella
   cheese
1 T. fresh parsley, chopped
1 T. oil

Gently remove mushroom stems; set aside caps. Chop stems and mix with shallot; set aside. Melt butter in a skillet over medium-high heat; add stem mixture. Sauté until stems are soft but not mushy and shallot is translucent. Stir in sherry; reduce heat to low and simmer for 3 minutes. In a bowl, combine stem mixture, bread crumbs, cheese and parsley; mix well. Use oil to coat a 13"x9" baking pan. Spoon mixture into mushroom caps; arrange in pan. Bake, uncovered, at 350 degrees for 20 to 25 minutes, until golden. Makes one dozen.

When buying a fresh tree, be sure to take home any boughs cut from the base of the tree. Nothing says Christmas like fresh touches of greenery sprinkled throughout your home!

Brown Sugar Dijon Bacon

Desirae Fear
Franklin, IN

I came across a recipe for Brown Sugar Bacon among my grandma's recipes. I added some Dijon mustard to cut the sweetness of the brown sugar...the result is delicious!

1 c. brown sugar, packed
1 T. Dijon mustard

8 slices bacon, cut in half
  crosswise

Mix together brown sugar and mustard in a shallow bowl. Coat bacon in mixture, one slice at a time. Arrange on a wire rack in an ungreased 13"x9" baking pan. Bake, uncovered, at 400 degrees for 20 minutes, or until crisp. Let stand 5 minutes before serving. Serves 8.

Golden Cheese Rounds

Donna Masson
Manchester, NH

I make this appetizer at Christmas Eve every year and the family looks forward to it. It's handy to have on hand in the freezer.

1 c. all-purpose flour
8-oz. pkg. shredded sharp
  Cheddar cheese

1/2 c. butter, softened
2 T. onion soup mix
1/2 t. salt

Combine all ingredients in a bowl; mix well. Form into 2 logs, each about one inch in diameter. Wrap logs in plastic wrap; freeze. To serve, remove from freezer; thaw slightly. Slice 1/4-inch thick; place on ungreased baking sheets. Bake at 375 degrees for 8 to 10 minutes, until golden. Serve warm. Serves 12 to 14.

I wish we could put up some of the Christmas spirit in jars
and open a jar of it every month.

–Harlan Miller

Cheese-Stuffed Celery

Lisanne Miller
Canton, MS

At the holidays, my grandmother always served celery stuffed with cream cheese and pimento. This is an updated recipe, a bit more savory and can be made a day ahead!

2 8-oz. pkgs. cream cheese, softened
1/4 c. onion-garlic jam or favorite chutney
2 T. shredded Cheddar cheese
2 t. pepper
1 bunch celery, trimmed into stalks

In a bowl, combine all ingredients except celery; mix until very smooth. Fill celery stalks with cheese mixture. Cover and refrigerate. At serving time, cut celery stalks into bite-size pieces. Serves 6 to 8.

Pecan-Stuffed Dates

Gladys Kielar
Whitehouse, OH

Your guests will love this old-fashioned appetizer.

10-oz. pkg. pitted dates
30 to 36 pecan halves
10 to 12 slices bacon, each cut into 3 pieces

Stuff each date with a pecan half. Wrap a piece of bacon around each stuffed date; secure with a wooden toothpick. Arrange on an ungreased baking sheet. Bake, uncovered, at 400 degrees until bacon is crisp, 12 to 15 minutes. Drain and serve. Makes about 2-1/2 dozen.

Send the kids outside with gelatin molds, ice cream scoops, cake and bread pans so they can create the best-ever snow fort.

Pecan Chicken Salad Spread

Amy Butcher
Columbus, GA

*We do love our pecans here in Georgia! This flavorful spread is
perfect for snacking or for making tea sandwiches.*

1-3/4 c. cooked chicken breast,
  finely chopped
1 c. chopped pecans
2/3 c. mayonnaise
1 stalk celery, chopped

1/2 c. onion, minced
1 t. salt
1/2 t. garlic powder
assorted crackers, French bread
  slices

In a bowl, combine all ingredients except crackers; mix well. Cover
and chill. Serve with crackers or bread slices. Makes 2-1/2 cups.

Make a party tray of savory appetizer tarts...guests will
love 'em. Bake frozen mini phyllo shells according to
package directions, then fill with a favorite creamy dip
or spread. Grandma never had it so easy!

46

Ambrosia Cheese Ball

Lisanne Miller
Canton, MS

Inspired by old-fashioned ambrosia salad, this updated cheese ball is great year 'round and you can serve it with something salty or sweet! It can be made 3 or 4 days ahead, chilled and ready to serve when guests arrive. For added flavor, top with crushed pineapple.

2 8-oz. pkgs. cream cheese, softened
1/4 c. shredded Cheddar cheese
1/2 c. orange marmalade or seedless raspberry jam
1/4 c. raisins
1/8 t. ground ginger
1/2 c. toasted flaked coconut
vanilla wafers or gingersnaps

In a large bowl, combine cheeses, marmalade or jam, raisins and ginger. Blend until well combined. Cover and chill overnight or up to 4 days. At serving time, form into a ball; roll in toasted coconut. Serve with vanilla wafers or gingersnaps. Makes 8 to 10 servings.

Turn vintage jelly glasses into candles. Holding a wick in place, pour scented wax candle gel into each glass. They're especially pretty with gels in glowing "jelly" colors like red and amber!

Phil's Famous Bean Dip

Jennifer Rose Blay
Puyallup, WA

When I was growing up, my stepdad Phil made this awesome bean dip for all of my birthday parties and our family get-togethers. It was always a big hit! Now I carry on the tradition. I added the jalapeño flavored cheese dip to give it an extra special kick.

16-oz. can refried beans
16-oz. jar favorite salsa
3 c. shredded Cheddar cheese

9-oz. can jalapeño Cheddar
cheese dip
tortilla chips

In a large microwave-safe bowl, combine all ingredients except tortilla chips. Mix well; cover with plastic wrap. Microwave on high setting until all of the cheese is melted, stirring after every minute. Serve warm with tortilla chips. Serves 8 to 10.

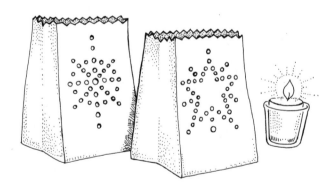

Warm and welcoming! Light the path with luminarias...
fill lunch bags about 1/3 full with sand, then nestle a votive
in each. Light just in time to greet your first guests.

Holiday Open House

Gram's Christmas Chili Dip

Sandy Coffey
Cincinnati, OH

This is an easy recipe to share on Christmas Eve while opening gifts and enjoying family time. It's a favorite that the kids ask for year after year.

2 8-oz. pkgs. cream cheese, softened
1 bunch green onions, finely chopped
1 to 2 10-oz. pkgs. frozen chili, thawed
2 8-oz. pkgs. shredded Colby cheese
saltine crackers

Spread cream cheese evenly in the bottom of an ungreased 13"x9" baking pan. Sprinkle green onions over cream cheese. Spoon desired amount of chili over top; sprinkle with shredded cheese. Bake, uncovered, at 350 degrees until hot and bubbly, about 10 to 15 minutes. Serve warm with crackers. Makes 12 servings.

Sparkling Christmas Punch

Elaine Miller
Waterville, OH

My family always had Mexican food on Christmas Eve. This festive, refreshing punch went so well with the meal.

3-oz. pkg. wild strawberry gelatin mix
1 c. boiling water
6-oz. can frozen pink lemonade concentrate, thawed
46-oz. can pineapple juice
3 c. cold water
2 ltrs. lemon-lime soda, chilled
ice cubes

Dissolve gelatin mix in boiling water; pour into a one-gallon jug or pitcher. Add lemonade, pineapple juice and cold water; stir well and chill. Just before serving, pour in soda and mix well. Serve over ice cubes. Makes 24 servings.

Frosty the Cheese Ball

R. E. Rohlof
Hicksville, OH

*Fun and tasty too! Garnish with sliced black olives for the eyes
and mouth, a baby carrot for the nose, red pepper triangles
for the buttons and pretzel stick arms.*

2 8-oz. pkgs. cream cheese,
  softened
1/4 c. mayonnaise
1 T. prepared horseradish
1/4 t. red pepper flakes
3-oz. jar bacon bits

1-1/4 c. chopped nuts
1/2 c. fresh parsley, finely
  chopped
2 green onions, finely chopped
assorted crackers

Combine all ingredients except crackers in a large bowl; mix very well.
Divide mixture into 3 balls, forming one small, one medium and one
large ball. Arrange the balls flat on a serving platter to form a
snowman. Cover and chill; serve with crackers. Serves 8 to 10.

Set aside time for a little crafting with friends. Choose a
favorite theme, like card and tag making, and everyone
can bring along their favorite supplies to share.

50

Parmesan Meatballs

Judith Levy
Sumner, WA

My mother gave me this delicious recipe over 50 years ago when I was first married. Everyone at our open houses raves about it. It's an easy make-ahead since the meatballs and sauce can be frozen.

1 lb. ground beef
1/2 c. dry bread crumbs
1/2 c. milk
1 egg, lightly beaten
1/2 c. grated Parmesan cheese
1 T. dried, minced onion
salt and pepper to taste
2 T. butter, sliced

1/4 c. all-purpose flour
4-oz. can mushroom stems & pieces
1 c. canned beef consommé or broth
1/2 c. sauterne wine or water
1/2 c. light cream

In a large bowl, combine beef, bread crumbs, milk, egg, cheese, onion, salt and pepper. Mix well; form into 1/2-inch meatballs. Melt butter in a large skillet over medium heat. Add meatballs; brown on all sides. Remove meatballs to a plate. Add flour to drippings in skillet; blend well. Add undrained mushrooms and remaining ingredients to skillet. Cook, stirring constantly, until thickened and smooth. Season with salt and pepper. Add meatballs to sauce in skillet; cover and simmer for 20 minutes. Serves 20.

To Freeze:

Package meatballs and sauce separately in freezer containers. To serve, thaw in the refrigerator. Simmer meatballs with sauce, as directed above.

A dish filled with whole walnuts, almonds and hazelnuts is a treat for visitors. Don't forget the nutcracker!

Girls' Night Buffalo Chicken Dip

Judy Davis
Muskogee, OK

This is a favorite of my girlfriends when we get together
for Craft Night. It's super good and so easy!

2 8-oz. pkgs. cream cheese,
  softened
3/4 c. mayonnaise
1 c. hot pepper sauce
1 T. garlic powder, or to taste
1 t. salt

1 t. pepper
3 8-oz. cans chicken breast,
  drained and flaked
8-oz. pkg. shredded mozzarella
  cheese, divided
crusty bread slices, crackers

In a large bowl, whisk together cream cheese with mayonnaise until smooth and creamy. Stir in hot sauce, seasonings, chicken and one cup mozzarella cheese. Spread in a lightly greased 9"x9" baking pan; top with remaining cheese. Bake, uncovered, at 350 degrees for 30 to 45 minutes, until heated through and cheese is golden. Serve warm with crusty bread and crackers. Serves 8 to 10.

A fondue pot is a must for keeping sweet & savory dips just right for serving. Simply fill the fondue pot, turn it to the warm setting and forget about it!

3-Cheese Artichoke Bread

Marcia Marcoux
Charlton, MA

*A tasty snack for a crowd...serve it as an appetizer
or alongside your favorite pasta dish.*

1/3 c. butter, sliced
1 T. garlic, minced
14-oz. can artichoke hearts,
  drained and chopped
1 c. shredded mozzarella cheese

1 c. grated Parmesan cheese
1/2 c. sour cream
salt and pepper to taste
1 loaf French bread
1/2 c. shredded Cheddar cheese

Melt butter in a skillet over medium-low heat. Add garlic and cook until fragrant, about 30 seconds. Add artichokes, mozzarella cheese, Parmesan cheese and sour cream; stir to blend. Remove skillet from heat. Season with salt and pepper; cool. Cut loaf in half lengthwise; scoop out some of the center. Spoon artichoke mixture evenly into bread shells; sprinkle with Cheddar cheese. Place halves on a baking sheet. Cover loosely with aluminum foil. Bake at 350 degrees for 25 minutes. Remove foil; bake for another 5 to 8 minutes, until cheese is completely melted. Slice and serve warm. Makes 8 to 10 servings.

Kids will love finding surprises tucked into old-fashioned Christmas crackers. Just fill cardboard tubes with an assortment of candies, trinkets and confetti. Wrap it all up in colorful paper and tie the ends up with ribbon.

Pinky Winks

Linda Knox
Niota, TN

This old-time recipe freezes well...very handy when you're preparing for a large holiday buffet.

1 lb. hot ground pork sausage
1 lb. ground beef
16-oz. pkg. pasteurized process
    cheese spread, cubed
4-oz. can sliced mushrooms,
    drained and diced

1 t. dried oregano
1 t. dried basil
1 t. garlic salt
1/4 t. pepper
1 t. Worcestershire sauce
2 loaves party rye bread

In a large skillet over medium heat, cook sausage and beef until browned, breaking up with a spatula. Drain; reduce heat to low. Add remaining ingredients except bread. Cook until cheese is melted, stirring often. Spread warm mixture thinly on bread slices. Arrange slices on ungreased baking sheets. Broil until bubbly and golden, watching carefully. Serves 8 to 10.

To Freeze:

Spread sausage mixture on bread slices; place on baking sheets and freeze. Remove frozen slices to plastic zipping bags; keep frozen. To serve, thaw in the refrigerator; broil as directed above.

For snow-day fun, pull out jigsaw puzzles, nostalgic games like checkers and dominoes or card games like Go Fish and Old Maid.

Cheesy Mushroom Spread

Goreta Brown
Calgary, Alberta

This scrumptious spread is really easy to make...try it and see!

6 to 8 slices bacon
2 T. butter
1 onion, chopped
8-oz. pkg. sliced mushrooms
2 T. all-purpose flour
8-oz. container sour cream

1 t. lemon juice
1/8 t. cayenne hot pepper sauce
2 c. shredded Cheddar cheese
crusty bread slices or snack
  crackers

In a skillet over medium heat, cook bacon until crisp; drain. Set bacon aside on a plate. Melt butter in same skillet. Add onion and cook until tender, about 2 minutes. Add mushrooms and cook until soft, about 2 minutes. Stir in flour; cook and stir until blended. Stir in sour cream, lemon juice and hot sauce; heat through. Spoon into a lightly greased 9" pie plate; top with cheese. Bake, uncovered, at 350 degrees for 20 to 25 minutes, until cheese is hot and bubbly. Serve with bread or crackers. Makes 8 to 10 servings.

Childhood toys add a feel of nostalgia to Christmas displays.
Sailboats, airplanes, teddy bears, dolls and tea sets all
bring back fond memories. Set them on tables, stairs,
cupboard shelves or mantels.

People Puppy Chow

M'lissa Johnson
Baytown, TX

This special treat is a must around our house for snacking at Christmas. The kids love to help me shake the paper bag, and the name makes everyone giggle.

9 c. bite-size crispy rice
cereal squares
1-3/4 c. powdered sugar

1-1/2 c. semi-sweet chocolate
chips
3/4 c. creamy peanut butter

Place cereal in a large heatproof bowl; set aside. Add powdered sugar to a separate large covered container or brown paper bag; set aside. Place chocolate chips in a microwave-safe bowl. Microwave for 30 seconds on high setting; stir and repeat until chips are melted. Stir in peanut butter until smooth. Pour chocolate mixture over cereal; stir until cereal is completely coated. Add cereal mixture to powdered sugar in bag; toss until well coated. Store in an airtight container. Makes about 12 cups.

Paper baking cups are perfect for serving up
party-size scoops of nuts or snack mix.

Becky's Favorite Glazed Walnuts
Rebecca Jahnke
Tracyton, WA

One day I found this among my grandmother's recipe cards and gave it a try. It was perfect for what I needed! Now it's a weakness for my friend Becky...my oldest daughter and I really like these nuts too. Their sweet simplicity has become a favorite!

1/2 c. margarine, sliced	1 t. cinnamon
1 c. brown sugar, packed	4 c. walnut halves

Place margarine in a microwave-safe 2-quart bowl. Microwave on high setting for one minute. Add brown sugar and cinnamon; microwave for 2 minutes. Add walnut halves and toss to coat. Microwave for 5 minutes. Spread nuts on a baking sheet; allow to cool. Store in an airtight container. Makes about 4 cups.

For as long as I can remember, my grandmother, mother and now my sisters, my daughters and I have used the Christmas cards we receive as a part of our holiday decorating. We tape them to the inside of the front door or on the banister for all to enjoy. I used to help Mom hang the cards, now I decorate my own home and my girls help me. After the holidays, we take the cards down and make Christmas gift tags or ornaments from them for next year.

–Janice Woods, Northern Cambria, PA

Praline Pecan & Cranberry Mix
Joyceann Dreibelbis
Wooster, OH

Delight your family and friends with this sweet and savory snack. It always wins rave reviews!

3-1/2 c. pecan halves
1/4 c. light brown sugar, packed
1/4 c. light corn syrup
2 T. butter, sliced

1 t. vanilla extract
1/4 t. baking soda
1-1/2 c. sweetened dried
  cranberries

Grease a 13"x9" baking pan. Spread pecans in a single layer in pan; set aside. Combine brown sugar, corn syrup and butter in a microwave-safe bowl. Microwave on high setting for one minute; stir. Microwave for 30 seconds to one minute more. Carefully stir in vanilla and baking soda until well blended. Drizzle evenly over pecans; stir until evenly coated. Bake, uncovered, at 250 degrees for one hour, stirring every 20 minutes with a wooden spoon. Cover a 15"x10" jelly-roll pan with heavy-duty aluminum foil. Immediately transfer mixture to prepared pan; spread pecans evenly with a lightly greased spatula. Cool completely; break pecans apart with a wooden spoon. Combine pecans and cranberries in a large bowl. Store in an airtight container at room temperature up to 2 weeks. Makes 5 cups.

Host a gift wrapping party! Gather up giftwrap, scissors and tape, play cheerful Christmas music and set out some snacks for nibbling. With everyone helping each other, you'll be done in a snap!

Rosemary Roasted Cashews

Lori Rosenberg
University Heights, OH

At our holiday family gatherings, happy hour is just as important as the festive meal. These nuts are a true crowd-pleaser, especially warm right out of the oven.

1-1/4 lbs. whole cashews
1 T. butter, melted
2 T. fresh rosemary, coarsely
   chopped

2 t. dark brown sugar, packed
2 t. kosher salt
1/2 t. cayenne pepper

Place cashews on an ungreased baking sheet. Bake at 375 degrees for about 10 minutes, until warmed through. Transfer warm nuts to a large bowl. Drizzle with melted butter; sprinkle with remaining ingredients. Toss until completely coated. Serve warm. Makes 3 cups.

Salted Roasted Pecans

Vicki Lanzendorf
Madison, WI

These simple nuts remind me of Grandma. She always served them at Christmas and it is a tradition I now carry on. I like to snack on them... they're also amazing sprinkled over a hot fudge sundae. They make great gifts if you don't eat them all yourself first!

5 T. butter, melted
1 lb. pecan halves

salt to taste

Spread melted butter in a rimmed baking sheet. Add pecans and stir to coat with butter; sprinkle with salt. Bake at 350 degrees for 10 minutes. Stir and add more salt, if desired. Return to oven for an additional 20 minutes. Cool completely. Keep refrigerated in an airtight container. Bring to room temperature before serving. Makes 4 cups.

Grandma's Cocktail Nibbles

Carolyn Deckard
Bedford, IN

Our large family used to gather at Grandma's every year on Christmas Eve to open presents. I can't believe it's been 60 years. Grandma would give us each a bag of this great snack. We still make it today, but Grandma's was best. Such good memories!

15-oz. pkg. bite-size crispy rice
    cereal squares
15-oz. pkg. doughnut-shaped
    oat cereal
6-oz. pkg. pretzel sticks, broken
    into small pieces
1 lb. salted peanuts
1 lb. cashews
1-1/2 c. butter, melted
1/4 c. Worcestershire sauce
3/4 T. garlic salt
3/4 T. onion salt
3/4 T. celery salt

Mix cereals, pretzels and nuts in a large roasting pan; set aside. Stir together remaining ingredients in a bowl. Drizzle over nut mixture and stir to mix thoroughly. Cover and bake at 225 degrees for one hour. Uncover and bake another hour, stirring occasionally. Spread out to to cool. Keeps almost indefinitely in an airtight container. Makes 12 to 15 servings.

When a snack mix recipe makes lots of servings, spoon it into a punch bowl and add a scoop. A stack of snack-size paper bags nearby will make it easy for everyone to help themselves.

All the
Trimmings

Cheesy Chicken Noodle Soup

Janet Myers
Reading, PA

This recipe was given to me by my 98-year-old mother.
It is simple and delicious, loved by all ages!

2 to 3 c. cooked chicken,
   shredded
4 to 6 c. chicken broth
10-3/4 oz. can Cheddar cheese
   soup

1 c. milk
1/2 c. fine egg noodles,
   uncooked
Optional: shredded Cheddar
   cheese

In a large stockpot, combine chicken, broth, soup and milk. Bring to a boil over medium heat, stirring occasionally. Reduce heat to medium-low; stir in noodles. Simmer until noodles are soft, about 5 minutes. Spoon into bowls. Sprinkle with cheese, if desired. Makes 6 to 8 servings.

I grew up in the 1960s. Each Christmas Eve we went to Granny's house for Christmas dinner with Daddy's extended family. We would gather around Granny for a family picture with everyone dressed in their best: red and white dresses and patent leather shoes on the girls, nice shirts and pants on the boys. Mama's hair would be fixed up with a wiglet on the top of her head that looked just like her real hair. Granny's enjoyment came from preparing food for us...more than we could eat! I didn't figure out why she made so much food until my own children left home...she liked to fix each child and grandchild's favorite foods. Granny felt rewarded when we told her how delicious our favorite dishes were. I didn't have a favorite, I loved anything she cooked!

– Ann Turner, Raleigh, NC

All the Trimmings

Gram's Simple Chili

Sandy Coffey
Cincinnati, OH

*This quick-to-fix chili is just the way my grandkids like...
chunky and mild tasting.*

1 lb. ground beef chuck
6-oz. can tomato paste
15-oz. can kidney beans
2 c. water

Garnish: saltine crackers,
　shredded Cheddar cheese,
　sour cream

Brown beef in a deep skillet over medium heat; drain. Add tomato paste and undrained beans; stir well. Add water. Reduce heat to medium-low and simmer for about 10 minutes, until well blended. Serve with crackers, sour cream and cheese. Serves 4.

Tuck a jar of hearty homemade soup into a big basket
alongside a stack of chunky pottery bowls...
a tummy-warming gift for a snowy day!

Yellow Pea Soup

Paulette Alexander
Saint George's, Newfoundland

While I was growing up, my mom made this soup every few weeks. It's still one of my favorites today and a tradition in Newfoundland.

2 c. cooked ham, chopped
8 c. cold water
2 c. dried yellow split peas
1 c. onion, chopped
1 c. turnip, peeled and diced

1 c. carrots, peeled and diced
2 to 3 potatoes, peeled and cubed
salt and pepper to taste

Combine ham and cold water in a large soup pot. Bring to a boil over medium heat; simmer for 30 minutes. Add peas and onion. Reduce heat to medium-low. Cover and simmer gently for one to 1-1/2 hours, stirring occasionally. Stir in remaining ingredients; cook until vegetables are tender, about 20 minutes. Makes 8 servings.

Beer Bread

Kim Hinshaw
Cedar Park, TX

When I was growing up, my grandma made yummy homemade bread. This version is quick & easy!

3 c. self-rising flour
12-oz. can regular or non-alcoholic beer, room temperature

1/4 c. sugar
1/2 c. butter, melted

Combine flour, beer and sugar in a large bowl. Stir just until moistened. Pour into a greased and floured 9"x5" loaf pan. Drizzle with melted butter. Bake at 375 degrees for 45 to 55 minutes. Serve warm. Makes one loaf.

A simmering kettle of soup fills the house with a wonderful aroma...so relaxing when you're wrapping gifts or writing Christmas cards.

Mom's Zucchini Soup

*Judy Henfey
Cibolo, TX*

This delicious recipe from my mom is what won my husband...Mom made it one night and he never left. Thanks, Mom! This soup tastes even better the following day.

1 lb. hot or sweet Italian pork
  sausage links, casings
  removed
2 c. celery, sliced 1/2-inch thick
  at an angle
2 28-oz. cans crushed tomatoes
2 lbs. zucchini, sliced 1/2-inch
  thick at an angle
1 c. onion, chopped
2 t. salt

1 t. Italian seasoning
1 t. dried oregano
1/2 t. dried basil
1/2 t. sugar
1/4 t. garlic powder
Optional: 2 green peppers,
  cut into 1/2-inch pieces
Garnish: grated Parmesan
  cheese

In a large soup pot over medium heat, brown sausage. Partially drain. Add celery and cook for 15 minutes, stirring frequently. Add tomatoes with juice, zucchini, onion and seasonings. Reduce heat to low. Cover and simmer for 20 to 30 minutes, stirring occasionally. Add peppers, if desired; cook for an additional 10 to 15 minutes. Sprinkle with Parmesan cheese. Makes 3-1/2 quarts.

Serve Mom's Zucchini Soup with toasty baguette chips. Thinly slice a loaf of French bread. Brush slices with olive oil; place on a baking sheet and sprinkle with grated Parmesan cheese. Bake at 350 degrees until crisp and golden, about 10 minutes.

Italian Sausage Soup

Eleanor Dionne
Beverly, MA

This is a wonderful cold-weather soup...chunky, flavorful and sustaining. We make a lot of soup in winter and Monday is our favorite day for soup. We enjoy this one in particular.

1 lb. sweet Italian pork sausage links, casings removed
1 onion, chopped
2 cloves garlic, chopped
28-oz. can Italian-style diced tomatoes
14-oz. can beef broth
3/4 c. dry red wine or beef broth

1-1/2 T. fresh parsley, minced
1/2 t. dried basil
1 zucchini, sliced
1/2 green pepper, chopped
2 c. large bow-tie pasta, uncooked
Garnish: grated Parmesan cheese

In a large soup pot over medium heat, sauté sausage, onion and garlic until sausage is browned. Drain; add tomatoes with juice, broth, wine or broth, parsley and basil. Reduce heat to medium-low. Cover and simmer for 30 minutes, stirring occasionally. Add zucchini and green pepper; simmer for another 15 to 20 minutes. Stir in uncooked pasta. Cook for 8 to 10 minutes, until pasta is tender. Top each serving with a sprinkle of Parmesan cheese. Serves 4 to 6.

Soups & stews stay nice and warm when spooned into a slow cooker that's turned to the low setting. This way, no matter when family, friends or neighbors arrive for a visit, the soup will be ready to enjoy.

Dad's Polish Bean Soup

Jessica Kraus
Delaware, OH

I grew up with this hearty soup. After any holiday where there was a ham for dinner, I knew Dad would be making this soup! This soup simmers for hours...perfect for a snowed-in weekend.

12 c. water
16-oz. pkg. dried 16-bean
  soup mix
1 meaty ham bone
1 lb. Kielbasa sausage, diced
1/2 lb. bacon, diced

2 c. celery, chopped
2 c. carrots, peeled and chopped
1 onion, diced
salt and pepper to taste
Optional: few drops smoke-
  flavored cooking sauce

Bring water to a boil in a large stockpot over high heat. Add bean mix and ham bone; reduce heat to medium-low. Cover and simmer for 2 hours, stirring occasionally. Meanwhile, brown sausage and cook bacon in separate skillets; drain on paper towels. When soup has simmered for 2 hours, remove ham bone; cool. Add sausage, bacon and remaining ingredients to soup. Cut ham off the bone and add to soup; discard bone. Return soup to a boil; reduce heat to medium-low and simmer for an additional 2 hours. Shortly before serving time, use a potato masher to partially mash the beans. This will make the soup thicker and heartier. Makes 10 servings.

Make time for your town's special holiday events. Whether it's a Christmas parade, Santa arriving by horse-drawn sleigh or a tree lighting ceremony, hometown traditions make the best memories!

Ruth's Creamy White Chicken Chili

Tamara Martindale
Solsberry, IN

My step-mom Ruth used to make this soup on Christmas Eve for everyone to enjoy. I never cared for it until I actually made it myself years later, now I love it! Thank you, Mom, for a wonderful recipe.

1 lb. boneless, skinless
   chicken breast, cut into
   1/2-inch cubes
1 T. oil
14-oz. can chicken broth
1 onion, chopped
2 15-1/2 oz. cans Great
   Northern beans, drained
   and rinsed
2 4-oz. cans chopped green
   chiles

1-1/2 t. garlic powder
1 t. ground cumin
1 t. dried oregano
1 t. salt
1/2 t. pepper
1/4 t. cayenne pepper
8-oz. container sour cream
1/2 c. whipping cream
Optional: shredded Cheddar
   cheese, salsa

In a stockpot over medium heat, sauté chicken in oil until golden; drain. Add remaining ingredients except sour cream, whipping cream and optional garnish. Bring to a boil; reduce heat to medium-low. Simmer, uncovered, for 30 minutes. Remove from heat; stir in sour cream and whipping cream just before serving. Top with Cheddar cheese and salsa, if desired. Serves 4.

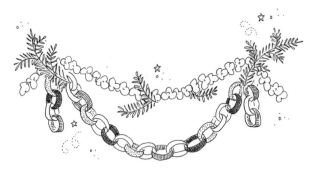

Enjoy a wintry day of play with your children. Build a snow fort, cut out paper snowflakes, string cranberries for the tree or bake and decorate cookies together. Memories in the making!

Spicy Garden Chili

JoAnn

*Mexican-style seasonings and two kinds of beans
make this meatless chili extra special.*

1 T. oil
1 c. onion, chopped
1 c. celery, sliced
1 t. garlic, minced
28-oz. can diced tomatoes
15-oz. can kidney beans,
  drained and rinsed
15-1/2 oz. can lima beans,
  drained and rinsed

1 c. vegetable broth
2 T. fresh basil, chopped
1 T. chili powder
1 t. sugar
1/2 t. ground cumin
1/4 t. cayenne pepper
Garnish: sour cream

Heat oil in a large saucepan over medium heat. Add onion, celery and garlic. Sauté for 3 to 4 minutes, until tender. Stir in tomatoes with juice and remaining ingredients except garnish. Cook, stirring often, until mixture comes to a full boil. Reduce heat to low. Cover and cook for 15 to 20 minutes, stirring occasionally. Garnish servings with a dollop of sour cream. Serves 6.

Cornbread and chili are made for each other! Shake up Grandmother's best cornbread recipe by adding some shredded Cheddar cheese, diced green chiles or fresh corn kernels.

Christy's Taco Soup

Christy Woosley
Bloomingdale, IL

This is an easy recipe to make either on the stovetop or in the slow cooker. Just brown, dump and warm...it's almost foolproof!

1 lb. ground beef
15-oz. can tomato sauce
15-1/2 oz. can kidney, pinto or
   Great Northern beans
14-1/2 oz. can diced tomatoes
15-oz. can sweet corn

1-1/4 oz. pkg. taco seasoning
   mix
Garnish: crushed tortilla chips,
   shredded Cheddar cheese,
   sour cream

Brown beef in a soup pot over medium heat; drain. Add tomato sauce, undrained vegetables and taco seasoning. Bring to a boil; reduce heat to low. Cover and simmer at least 20 minutes, stirring occasionally. The longer the soup simmers, the better the flavor will be. May also combine all ingredients except garnish in a slow cooker; cover and cook on low setting for 6 to 8 hours. Serve with crushed tortilla chips, cheese and a dollop of sour cream mixed into each bowl. Serves 5.

Wondering what to do with Grandma's button box?
Hot glue buttons to a wreath form for a fun wreath. Try
using different shades of all red, green or white for an
even more eye-catching design.

Country Cornbread

Glenda Bolton
Dandridge, TN

My mother made this cornbread for as long as I can remember.
She cooked it in a pan on top of the stove. My only change is
that I bake mine in a cast-iron skillet in the oven.

5 T. oil, divided
2 c. self-rising cornmeal
3/4 c. self-rising flour

2 c. buttermilk
2 eggs, beaten

Brush a 9" to 10" cast-iron skillet generously with one tablespoon oil. Set oven to 450 degrees; place skillet on a rack in center of oven. Meanwhile, in a large bowl, stir together cornmeal and flour; make a well in the center. In a separate bowl, whisk together buttermilk, eggs and remaining oil. Pour buttermilk mixture into the well in cornmeal mixture; stir just until moistened. Carefully remove hot skillet from oven; pour in batter. Bake at 450 degrees for 15 to 20 minutes, until cornbread springs back when pressed in the center. Let stand for 5 minutes; turn cornbread out onto a plate or serve directly from the skillet. Makes 8 servings.

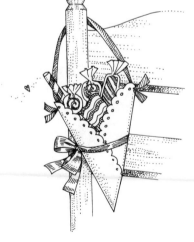

A charming welcome! Fill Victorian-style paper cones
with old-fashioned hard candies and hang from
chair backs with ribbons.

71

Mushroom-Barley Soup

Carole Clark
Sterling Heights, MI

So easy, so budget-friendly and ohhh-so tasty! A delicious way to use up leftover mushrooms, even if they're a little wrinkled. Serve with a crisp salad and some crusty bread for a very satisfying meal in cold weather.

1 T. canola or olive oil
1/2 c. onion, diced
1 stalk celery, diced
1 carrot, peeled and diced
10 to 12 white mushrooms,
    sliced

32-oz. container beef broth
1/4 c. long-cooking barley,
    uncooked
pepper to taste

Heat oil in a soup pot over medium heat. Add onion, celery and carrot; sauté for several minutes, until tender. Add mushrooms; sauté until softened. Add remaining ingredients; bring to a boil. Reduce heat to low. Cover and simmer for one to 1-1/2 hours, stirring occasionally, until barley is tender. Makes 3 to 4 servings.

Pass along Grandma's soup tureen to a new bride...
fill it with favorite seasonings and tie on a
cherished soup recipe.

All the Trimmings

Creamy Broccoli Soup

Robin Hill
Rochester, NY

Serve small cups of this smooth and satisfying soup as a meal starter.

2-1/2 c. water
1 cube chicken bouillon
1/2 lb. broccoli, chopped
1 c. celery, chopped

1/3 c. onion, chopped
5-oz. can evaporated milk
1/2 t. pepper
1/2 c. cream cheese, softened

In a saucepan over medium-high heat, combine water and bouillon. Bring to a boil; stir until bouillon dissolves. Reduce heat to medium. Add vegetables; cover and simmer until soft, about 15 to 20 minutes. Working in batches, purée soup in a blender until smooth. Return soup to saucepan over low heat; stir in evaporated milk and pepper. Just before serving, add cream cheese. Stir until well blended. Serves 6.

Crazy Quilt Bread

Lisanne Miller
Canton, MS

Growing up, when my mother made this bread, we knew Christmas was upon us! It's the first recipe I can remember baking with her and my grandmother. Serve warm with flavored butter.

1 egg, beaten
1-1/4 c. milk
1/2 c. sugar
3 c. biscuit baking mix
3/4 t. almond extract

1/2 c. mixed candied fruit, chopped
3/4 c. walnuts, pecans or almonds, coarsely chopped

In a bowl, stir together egg, milk, sugar and biscuit mix. Beat vigorously by hand for 30 seconds. Batter will be slightly lumpy. Blend in extract, fruit and nuts. Pour batter into a well-greased 9"x5" loaf pan. Bake at 350 degrees for 45 to 50 minutes, until a toothpick inserted in center tests clean. Cool before slicing; serve warm. Makes one loaf.

Fast & Festive Dinner Salad

Peggy Donnally
Toledo, OH

*A colorful and healthy salad that's perfect for wintertime,
since the ingredients are available year 'round.*

1 head romaine lettuce, torn
   into bite-size pieces
3/4 c. sweetened dried
   cranberries
3/4 c. crumbled blue cheese

1/2 c. red onion, diced
1/4 c. sunflower seed kernels
favorite poppy seed salad
   dressing to taste

Combine all ingredients except salad dressing in a serving bowl.
Drizzle with salad dressing; toss to mix. Serves 4.

Nancy's Poppy Seed Dressing

Nancy Toler
Dover, DE

*I used to do a lot of cooking outside my home and this recipe
was always requested. It's delicious on fruit or tossed salad.
Folks just loved this dressing and you will also!*

2 c. salad oil
2/3 c. cider vinegar
1/2 c. sugar, or 12 envs. calorie-
   free powdered sweetener

2 T. poppy seed
2 T. onion, finely chopped
2 t. dry mustard
2 t. salt

Combine all ingredients in a covered blender. Process until thoroughly
mixed. Store in refrigerator in a covered one-quart jar. Shake well prior
to using. Makes about 3 cups.

Cut snowflakes from folded paper...better yet,
show the kids how to do it. Scatter your creations
around the dining table...delightful!

Aunt Fifi's Spinach Salad

Judy Loemker
Edwardsville, IL

This recipe has been a family favorite for decades. Everyone loves the Parmesan Dressing! Aunt Fifi and Uncle Leo were among our wonderful aunts and uncles who used to host holiday get-togethers for our large clan. I always get compliments when serving this salad. Hope you'll try it, too!

10-oz. bag spinach, torn into
    bite-size pieces
2 to 3 eggs, hard-boiled,
    peeled and sliced

2 c. cherry tomatoes, halved
1-1/2 c. sliced mushrooms
1 onion, thinly sliced

Combine all ingredients in a large salad bowl. Pour 1/2 cup Parmesan Dressing over salad and toss well. Serve immediately. Serves 6 to 8.

Parmesan Dressing:

3/4 c. canola oil
1/4 c. lemon juice
3 T. grated Parmesan cheese,
    or more to taste

1 clove garlic, pressed
1-1/2 t. paprika
3/4 t. salt
1/4 t. sugar

Make dressing ahead of time by shaking all ingredients together in a covered jar. Chill before using. Makes about one cup.

For a cheery winter welcome, fill a child's wagon with poinsettias and place by the front door.

Warm Orzo Salad

Phyl Broich-Wessling
Garner, IA

*This is a favorite dish, colorful and simple to make. It is wonderful
as a side for pork chops. Serve on lettuce-lined salad plates,
garnished with cherry tomatoes and a sprinkle of pine nuts.*

16-oz. pkg. orzo pasta,
　uncooked
12-oz. jar roasted red peppers,
　drained and large pieces
　cut up
3-1/2 oz. jar capers, drained

14-oz. jar artichoke hearts,
　drained
6-oz. can black olives, drained
　and halved
1 c. pine nuts

Cook orzo according to package directions. Drain; transfer orzo to a
serving bowl. Mix in remaining ingredients. Toss with desired amount
of Olive Oil Dressing. Serve warm. Serves 10 to 15.

Olive Oil Dressing:

1/2 to 3/4 c. olive oil
juice of 1/2 lemon
2 T. garlic, minced

1 T. fresh oregano, chopped,
　or to taste
2 t. fresh parsley, chopped

Make dressing ahead of time by shaking all ingredients together in a
covered jar. Cover and chill before using.

Fresh scents for the holidays! Pierce
small holes in oranges using a
toothpick, then fill each hole with
a whole clove. Tie a ribbon all the
way around, leaving a loop for hanging
on a doorknob or the Christmas tree.

Mom's Easy Cheesy Garlic Bread

*Cris Goode
Mooresville, IN*

*My mom always made this garlic bread for our family's Spaghetti Night.
Now I make it for my daughter, much to her delight!*

1 loaf Italian bread, sliced into
   12 pieces
1/2 c. butter, softened

garlic powder to taste
2 c. shredded mozzarella cheese

Spread bread slices on one side with butter; place on baking sheets.
Sprinkle bread with garlic powder; top with cheese. Broil for 2 to
3 minutes, until bread is toasted and cheese is melted. Makes
12 servings.

When I was growing up, each year my mother strung popcorn
to place on our Christmas tree. We would also bake gingerbread
men which we decorated, wrapped in plastic wrap, tied with
ribbon and carefully placed on our tree. It was a beautiful sight!
I carried on these traditions as my daughters were growing up.
I still string popcorn every year and place it on my tree.
Occasionally a cookie will get placed on the tree too, but the
popcorn has to go on there every year! My kids tease me and
call it my "Poor Man's Garland," but to me it represents a little
bit of my past. I thread my needle, put on a Christmas movie
and string a fresh batch of popcorn to complete my yearly
tradition. The popcorn just gives the tree that
extra warm, cozy country feeling.

–Cassie Hooker, La Porte, TX

Pickled Christmas Beets & Eggs

Missy Abbott
Hickory, PA

Mom and I have made this recipe together since I was a little girl. I still ask if she will be serving the pickled beets for Christmas, and of course she says yes! The cloves give them such a wonderful taste.

1/4 c. water
1/3 c. vinegar
1/4 c. sugar
1/2 t. cinnamon
1/4 t. ground cloves

1/4 t. salt
2 c. canned sliced beets, drained
and 2 T. beet juice reserved
6 eggs, hard-boiled and peeled

In a large saucepan, combine water, vinegar, sugar, spices and salt. Bring to a boil over medium heat; stir until sugar dissolves. Add beets and reserved beet juice. Reduce heat to medium-low; simmer for 5 minutes. Remove from heat; cool. Transfer beets and liquid to a non-metallic bowl. Add whole hard-boiled eggs, pushing them down into liquid. Cover and refrigerate for several hours. Serve with a slotted spoon. Makes 8 servings.

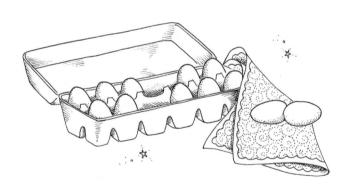

Try this for perfect hard-boiled eggs every time. Cover eggs with water in a saucepan; bring to a boil. Remove pan from heat, cover and let stand for 18 to 20 minutes. Immediately plunge the eggs into ice water and peel.

All the Trimmings

Crisp Cucumber Salad

Sandra Levine
Pembroke Pines, FL

*This is my grandmother's Hungarian recipe, brought over
more than a hundred years ago.*

10 small pickling cucumbers,
   peeled and very thinly sliced
1 onion, very thinly sliced and
   separated into rings
1/4 c. sugar

1/2 c. white vinegar
1/2 c. water
2 T. oil
salt and pepper to taste

Combine cucumbers and onion in a large bowl; set aside. In a small
bowl, combine sugar, vinegar, water and oil; stir until sugar dissolves.
Pour sugar mixture over cucumber mixture. Season with salt and
pepper. For best flavor, cover tightly and refrigerate at least 8 hours to
overnight. Serve with a slotted spoon. Serves 8.

When we recall Christmas past, we usually find that
the simplest things, not the great occasions,
give off the greatest glow of happiness.

– Bob Hope

Festive Broccoli & Cauliflower Salad
Beckie Apple
Grannis, AR

My family loves this salad! The dried cranberries give it a holiday meal feel anytime. Great for potluck dinners too.

2 12-oz. pkgs. broccoli &
 cauliflower salad mix
1 red onion, chopped
1 c. sweetened dried cranberries
1/2 c. bacon bits

1/2 c. plus 1 T. mayonnaise
1/2 c. sugar or powdered
 calorie-free sweetener
1 T. ranch salad dressing mix
1/4 t. coarse pepper

Place salad mix in a large serving bowl. Break broccoli and cauliflower into bite-size pieces, as needed. Add onion, cranberries and bacon bits; toss to mix well and set aside. In a small bowl, combine mayonnaise, sugar or sweetener, salad dressing mix and pepper; blend well. Add mayonnaise mixture to broccoli mixture; toss to coat well. Cover and chill for one to 2 hours before serving. Serves 6 to 8.

Gather up the neighbor kids and go caroling around the neighborhood...just for the joy of singing together! Make up pages with lyrics, or stick to favorites like "Jingle Bells" and "Deck the Halls" that everybody is sure to know.

Jane's Jingle Bell Cranberry Bread

Judy Henfey
Cibolo, TX

Every year, as soon as Thanksgiving dinner was over, Mom and Dad brought out the decorations and began transforming our home into a winter wonderland! Our manger scene went up first...our most prized pieces. Mom was born on Christmas morning, and she loved sharing her birthday with our Savior. This bread was one of her favorites and she always baked a loaf that day. Sweet memories!

1 c. all-purpose flour
1/4 c. sugar
1 t. baking powder
1/4 t. baking soda
1/4 t. salt

1 egg, beaten
2 T. canola oil
1 c. jellied cranberry sauce
1/2 c. golden raisins

In a bowl, mix flour, sugar, baking powder, baking soda and salt; set aside. In a separate large bowl, stir together egg, oil and cranberry sauce. Gradually add flour mixture to cranberry mixture; stir in raisins. Pour batter into a greased 9"x5" loaf pan. Bake at 350 degrees for 45 minutes, or until lightly golden. Makes one loaf.

Silent night, holy night.
All is calm, all is bright.

–Joseph Mohr

Holiday Fruit Salad

Audra LeNormand
Liberty, TX

Mom made this recipe for Christmas when I was growing up. Now her memory is sketchy, so I make it. She's always loved the holidays and family gatherings...she just loves people! Mom is now 86 and I feel blessed to still have both my parents.

16-oz. container frozen whipped
   topping, thawed
1/2 c. sour cream
30-oz. can fruit cocktail, drained
16-oz. container small-curd
   cottage cheese

1 firm banana, sliced
1/2 c. sweetened flaked coconut
3-oz. pkg. strawberry gelatin
   mix
1 c. mini marshmallows

Combine whipped topping and sour cream in a bowl; set aside. In a separate large bowl, combine fruit cocktail and cottage cheese. Add banana, coconut and dry gelatin mix; stir well. Add topping mixture; blend well. Fold in marshmallows. Cover and refrigerate overnight. Makes 8 to 10 servings.

With houses decorated for the holidays, it's a great time to host a progressive dinner! Enjoy appetizers at one home, then visit other homes for the soup, main course and dessert.

All the Trimmings

Frozen Cranberry Salad

Joanne Treynor
Chandler, AZ

This recipe has been in our family over 60 years and we make it every Thanksgiving and Christmas. We all love it!

12-oz. pkg. fresh cranberries
1/2 c. sugar
10-oz. pkg. mini marshmallows

15-1/4 oz. can crushed
  pineapple
1 pt. whipping cream

Grind cranberries in a food grinder or food processor; do not drain. Combine cranberries and sugar in a bowl; let stand for 2 hours. Stir in marshmallows and pineapple with juice; set aside. In a separate bowl, with an electric mixer on high speed, whip cream until soft peaks form. Add to cranberry mixture; stir well. Transfer to a serving bowl. Cover tightly with plastic wrap, then aluminum foil. Freeze for 3 days. Before serving, thaw in refrigerator all day. Serves 14 to 16.

Ginger-Orange Cranberries

Teresa Grimsley
Alamosa, CO

I promise that once you try this, it will become a part of your family's holiday tradition. It is very quick and can be prepared days in advance.

12-oz. pkg. fresh cranberries
1-1/3 c. sugar
1 c. orange juice
1 T. orange zest

1 T. fresh ginger, peeled and
  finely minced
Optional: cinnamon to taste

Combine all ingredients in a saucepan over medium heat. Cook, stirring often, until cranberries pop, 10 to 15 minutes. Immediately skim off any foam. Pour mixture into a serving bowl; allow to cool. Mixture will thicken and set as it cools. Cover and refrigerate up to 7 days. Makes 8 to 10 servings.

Baked Sweet Potatoes & Nutmeg Butter *JoAnn*

Sweet brown sugar and spicy nutmeg are sure to make this a new favorite in your family. So simple to do...the Nutmeg Butter can be made ahead of time and tucked in the fridge.

6 to 8 sweet potatoes

Line a baking sheet with heavy-duty aluminum foil; spray with non-stick vegetable spray. Arrange sweet potatoes on baking sheet. Bake at 350 degrees for one to 1-1/2 hours, until fork-tender. Remove from oven. Cut an X in the top of each sweet potato; press open and fluff pulp. Serve sweet potatoes topped with desired amount of Nutmeg Butter. Makes 6 to 8 servings.

Nutmeg Butter:

1/2 c. butter, softened
1/2 c. brown sugar, packed

3/4 t. nutmeg

Combine all ingredients in a bowl. Beat with an electric mixer on medium speed until light and fluffy. Cover; keep refrigerated.

Take a child to the grocery store to help choose holiday dinner ingredients with all the fixings to drop off at a local food pantry...a tradition well worth keeping.

All the Trimmings

Simple Sautéed Spinach

Sharon Tillman
Hampton, VA

Grandma always told us kids, "Eat your greens!" I think she'd be pleased with this recipe for zesty, fresh spinach.

2 T. extra-virgin olive oil
4 cloves garlic, thinly sliced
20-oz. pkg. fresh spinach
1 T. lemon juice

1/4 t. salt
Optional: 1/4 t. red pepper
flakes

Heat oil in a large skillet over medium heat. Add garlic; cook just until golden, one to 2 minutes. Add spinach; toss to coat. Cover and cook until soft, 3 to 5 minutes. Remove from heat. Add lemon juice, salt and red pepper flakes, if using. Toss to coat. Serves 4 to 6.

Herbed Fried Cauliflower

Angie Salayon
New Orleans, LA

This is a fast and delicious recipe. Serve it as a vegetable side or on a party tray with your favorite dip.

1 lb. fresh or frozen cauliflower
flowerets
1-oz. pkg. Italian or ranch salad
dressing mix

1 c. dry bread crumbs
2 eggs
oil for frying
salt to taste

Add cauliflower to a saucepan of boiling water. Cook for 8 to 14 minutes, just until tender. Drain well; pat dry with paper towels. In a shallow dish, combine salad dressing mix and bread crumbs. Beat eggs in a separate dish. Roll cauliflower in crumb mixture, then in egg, then in crumb mixture again. Heat 1/2 inch of oil in a skillet over medium heat. Cook cauliflower in batches until very lightly golden on both sides. Drain on paper towels; season with salt. Serves 4 to 6.

Sprinkle a tossed green salad with ruby-red
pomegranate seeds for a festive touch.

Cheesy Cauliflower Casserole
Michelle Powell
Valley, AL

This easy side tastes like a loaded baked potato!

2 lbs. fresh or frozen cauliflower
    flowerets
16-oz. pkg. shredded Colby Jack
    cheese, divided
8-oz. container plain Greek
    yogurt
1/4 c. milk

1 bunch green onions, thinly
    sliced
6 slices bacon, crisply cooked
    and crumbled
1 clove garlic, pressed
salt and pepper to taste

Add cauliflower to a saucepan of boiling water. Cook for 8 to
14 minutes, just until tender. Drain well; mash slightly with a potato
masher. Meanwhile, in a bowl, blend 3 cups cheese, yogurt and milk.
Stir in onions, bacon and garlic. Add cheese mixture to cauliflower;
stir well. Season with salt and pepper. Spoon into a greased 2-quart
casserole dish; top with remaining cheese. Cover with aluminum foil.
Bake at 350 degrees for 25 minutes. Uncover; bake until cheese is
bubbly, about 5 minutes. Makes 6 to 8 servings.

Before covering a favorite cheese-topped dish with aluminum
foil, be sure to spray the foil with non-stick vegetable spray...
the cheese won't stick when it melts.

All the Trimmings

Granny's Baked Macaroni & Cheese

Missy Staszewski
South Bend, IN

This was always one of my grandmother's favorite recipes to make for us as kids growing up. She was the best cook ever.

8-oz. pkg. elbow macaroni, uncooked
16-oz. pkg. mild Cheddar or Colby cheese, cubed
2 eggs, lightly beaten
1-1/2 c. milk
6 slices bacon, crisply cooked, crumbled and drippings reserved
salt and pepper to taste

Cook macaroni according to package directions; drain. In a large bowl, combine cooked macaroni, cheese, eggs, milk and bacon with reserved drippings. Season with salt and pepper; stir until well mixed. Spoon into a lightly greased 13"x9" glass baking pan. Cover and bake at 400 degrees for 30 minutes. Remove from oven; stir gently. Bake, uncovered, another 15 to 20 minutes, until golden and cheese is melted. Makes 8 to 10 servings.

A loving gift for your child straight from the heart...assemble a recipe box with all of Grandma's and Mom's favorite family recipes. Add new recipes each year along with funny little notes and sayings. A warm, wonderful gift to grow right along with your child...truly a box full of memories!

Cronins' Sage Dressing

Pat Martin
Riverside, CA

Our family has been enjoying this holiday dressing since the 50s...it's been my job to make it since 1972. I always double the recipe to make sure we have plenty of leftovers to share. I've even made it vegan-friendly for our son by substituting vegan butter and vegetable broth and it's still excellent. So simple, yet so good!

20 c. dry bread cubes	1-1/2 c. onion, diced
3 T. dried parsley	1-1/2 c. celery, diced
1 t. chicken bouillon granules	1 T. ground sage
3/4 c. boiling water	2 t. salt
1 c. butter, sliced	

In a very large bowl, combine bread cubes and parsley; set aside. Dissolve bouillon in boiling water; set aside. Place butter in an 8-cup glass measuring cup. Microwave on high until melted, one to 2 minutes. Add onion, celery, sage, salt and bouillon mixture. Microwave until vegetables are tender, 10 to 12 minutes. Pour over bread cube mixture; mix gently. Spoon into a buttered 13"x9" baking pan. Bake at 350 degrees for 30 to 34 minutes, until heated through and golden on top. May also be used to stuff a large turkey, up to 20 pounds; roast as preferred. Makes 10 servings.

Grandma never tossed out day-old bread and neither should you!
It keeps its texture better than very fresh bread...it's thrifty too.
Cut it into cubes, pack into freezer bags and freeze for making
stuffing cubes, casserole toppings and herbed salad croutons.

Pattersons' Potato Casserole
JoAlice Patterson-Welton
Lawrenceville, GA

This is such an easy and delicious side dish. My mom, who was a wonderful southern cook, used to make this in the fall and winter whenever she baked a beef tenderloin.

4 to 6 baking potatoes, peeled
   and sliced
1 onion, sliced
10-3/4 oz. can cream of
   chicken soup

1/2 c. milk
1/4 c. butter, melted
salt and pepper to taste

Layer potato and onion slices in a greased 3-quart casserole dish; set aside. In a bowl, mix together remaining ingredients; spoon over top. Bake, uncovered, at 375 degrees for one hour, or until potatoes are tender and golden. Makes 4 to 6 servings.

Small, blown-glass ornaments make charming party favors.
Tie them onto napkin rings with colorful ribbon...add a tag
with each guest's name on it.

Roasted Sweet Potatoes & Apples *Anne Alesauskas*
Minocqua, WI

I'll prepare this dish ahead of time before a big family meal.
Shortly before serving time, I top it with a pat of butter and
re-warm in the oven...oh my, it's heavenly!

2 to 3 sweet potatoes, peeled
    and cut into 1-inch cubes
2 T. extra-virgin olive oil,
    divided
1/2 t. cinnamon
1/2 t. cayenne pepper
salt to taste

3 Granny Smith apples, peeled,
    cored and diced
juice of 1/2 lemon
1 sprig fresh rosemary, finely
    chopped
1/2 c. pecans, coarsely chopped

In a large bowl, toss sweet potatoes with one tablespoon olive oil,
spices and salt. Spread on an ungreased baking sheet. Bake at
350 degrees for about 30 minutes, until very soft. Meanwhile, in a
separate bowl, toss apples with remaining oil, lemon juice, rosemary
and salt. Spread apples on a separate baking sheet. Bake at
350 degrees for 10 minutes. Sprinkle apples with pecans; bake an
additional 5 minutes. Transfer sweet potatoes to a serving bowl;
mash with a potato masher. Stir in apple mixture. Serves 6.

Dress up homemade or brown & serve dinner rolls...it's easy.
Before baking, brush the dough with a little beaten egg,
then sprinkle with sesame seed, dried rosemary or
grated Parmesan cheese.

Maple-Glazed Acorn Squash Rings *Gloria Simmons*
Greenville, MI

This is a wonderful side dish for a holiday dinner.

2 acorn squash, sliced crosswise
    into rings and seeds removed
salt and pepper to taste
1 c. maple syrup

1 tart apple, peeled, cored
    and chopped
1 t. cinnamon

Place squash rings in a greased 13"x9" baking pan; season with salt
and pepper. Combine remaining ingredients in a bowl; pour over
squash. Bake, uncovered, at 350 degrees for 40 to 60 minutes, until
squash is fork-tender. Makes 6 servings.

A cheery, painted chalkboard is ideal for kids as they
count down the days until Christmas.

German Sweet-and-Sour Red Cabbage

Gloria Simmons
Greenville, MI

This is my grandmother's old family recipe. Whenever she sat down to a Sunday or holiday dinner, there would be red cabbage on the table. I have fond memories of going to her loving home for the holidays... the aroma of red cabbage filled her kitchen.

2 to 2-1/2 lbs. red cabbage, chopped
1 apple, peeled, cored and finely diced
1/4 c. onion, finely chopped

1 c. water
6 T. brown sugar, packed
6 T. balsamic vinegar
2 T. bacon drippings

Combine all ingredients in a large saucepan. Bring to a boil over medium heat. Reduce heat to low; simmer for 30 to 45 minutes, stirring occasionally, until cabbage is tender and liquid has evaporated. Makes 8 servings.

Wrap up odd-shaped gifts in a jiffy...just use fabric!
Try red & green dots or a vintage novelty print for fun.
Tie with ribbon to match.

All the Trimmings

Easy Baked Artichokes

Paula Purcell
Plymouth Meeting, PA

A simple spin on stuffed artichokes that's fast and tasty.

2 8-1/2 oz. cans quartered
   artichokes, drained
1/4 c. olive oil
salt and pepper to taste

3/4 c. seasoned dry bread
   crumbs
3/4 c. grated Parmesan cheese

Place artichokes in a one-quart casserole dish sprayed with non-stick vegetable spray. Drizzle artichokes with olive oil; season with salt and pepper. Sprinkle bread crumbs and cheese on top. Bake, uncovered, at 375 degrees for 20 to 25 minutes, until golden. Makes 4 servings.

It's as much fun as you remember...
come on, make snow angels!

My Mom's Baked Beans

Nancy Kailihiwa
Wheatland, CA

When I was growing up, Mom made everything from scratch, just as her mom taught her and she taught me. I'm looking forward to handing down this recipe to my children some day.

1/2 lb. bacon
28-oz. can pork & beans
2 stalks celery, chopped

1/2 c. onion, finely chopped
1/4 c. catsup
1/2 c. brown sugar, packed

In a skillet over medium heat, cook bacon until crisp. Drain on paper towels; chop coarsely. In a large bowl, combine remaining ingredients and mix well. Add bacon; stir gently. Transfer to a well greased 2-quart casserole dish. Bake, uncovered, at 350 degrees for one hour, until beans are a rich brown and liquid has evaporated. Serves 4 to 6.

Lois's Baked Beans

Sandy Perry
Bakersfield, CA

This is an easy recipe from my mother-in-law. Great served hot with a meal or cold with a picnic!

32-oz. can pork & beans
1 c. brown sugar, packed
2 T. dry mustard

2 T. smoke-flavored cooking
   sauce

Mix together undrained beans and remaining ingredients in a bowl. Transfer to a greased one-quart bean pot or casserole dish. Bake, uncovered, at 350 degrees for one hour, until hot and bubbly. Makes 4 to 6 servings.

Small cheer and great welcome make a merry feast!
–William Shakespeare

All the Trimmings

Mashed Potato Filling Casserole
Mary Donaldson
Enterprise, AL

My dear friend Suzie is of Pennsylvania Dutch heritage. This is her mom's favorite potato recipe and a big part of her family's holiday gatherings. It has become one of my favorites too.

4 c. soft bread cubes
1/2 c. butter, sliced
1/2 c. celery, chopped
2 T. onion, chopped
1/2 c. boiling water

3 eggs, beaten
2 c. milk
1-1/2 t. salt
1/2 t. pepper
2 c. mashed potatoes

Place bread cubes in a heatproof bowl; set aside. Melt butter in a small saucepan over medium heat. Add celery and onion; cook until tender. Pour mixture over bread cubes; mix well. Add remaining ingredients; mix well after each addition. Mixture will be moist. Divide between 2 well greased one-quart casserole dishes. Bake, uncovered, at 350 degrees for 45 minutes. Serves 8 to 10.

Are the kids too excited on Christmas Day to sit down for a formal dinner? Set out a make-ahead buffet of sliced baked ham or roast turkey, rolls or bread and a favorite side dish warming in a slow cooker. For dessert, a platter of Christmas cookies, of course. Relax...you'll enjoy the day too!

Grandma Rose's Walnut Bread

Phyllis Peters
Three Rivers, MI

*My grandmother would make tea sandwiches with her homemade
quick bread whenever we girls wanted a special treat.
We were never disappointed!*

2 c. milk
1 egg, beaten
1 t. vanilla extract
3-1/2 c. all-purpose flour
1/2 c. sugar

2 t. baking powder
1 c. black walnuts, chopped
Optional: softened butter,
   lettuce leaves

Whisk together milk, egg and vanilla in a bowl. In a separate large
bowl, mix flour, sugar and baking powder. Add flour mixture to milk
mixture; stir until moistened. Fold in walnuts. Pour batter into
2 greased 9"x5" baking pans. Let stand for a few minutes. Bake at
325 degrees for one hour. Cool; slice. If desired, serve with butter
and lettuce for tea sandwiches. Makes 2 loaves.

Pair a loaf of warm bread with a crock of fruit butter...yum!
Simply blend 1/2 cup each of softened butter and
strawberry or apricot preserves.

All the Trimmings

Laurie's Lemon Bread

Laurie Rupsis
Aiken, SC

Someone once told me this recipe should be included on my resume! It's supposed to taste even better after sitting for a day. Good luck with that...mine has never lasted that long, as my husband can eat the whole loaf! By the way, 3 tablespoons lemon extract may seem like a lot, but trust me, that's correct.

1-1/2 c. sugar, divided
1/3 c. butter, melted
3 T. lemon extract
2 eggs, beaten
1/2 c. milk

1-1/2 c. all-purpose flour
1 t. baking powder
1-1/2 t. lemon zest
Optional: 1/2 c. chopped nuts
1/4 c. lemon juice

In a large bowl, mix one cup sugar and remaining ingredients except lemon juice. Pour batter into a greased and floured 9"x5" loaf pan. Bake at 350 degrees for 50 to 60 minutes. Cool 10 minutes; turn out loaf onto a piece of aluminum foil. For glaze, stir together lemon juice and remaining sugar. Drizzle glaze over loaf. For best flavor, wrap loaf in foil or plastic wrap; let stand one day before slicing. Makes one loaf.

Growing up, we didn't have extravagant Christmas gifts, as money was tight. We did, however, have a large extended family who gathered at Grandpa Toscano's home on Christmas Eve for a celebration. It was time to play with our cousins and of course, to eat great Italian food. One year, when we arrived back home, my two brothers and I found Santa filling our stockings...I remember being stunned and thrilled! Years later, I found out it was Mom's cousin Guido who dressed as Santa. What a wonderful memory!

–Laurene Shewan, Uncasville, CT

Christmas Mincemeat Muffins

Janis Parr
Campbellford, Ontario

*This is a moist, delicious muffin. The batter can be made
ahead and stored for up to two weeks in the fridge,
which is so handy at Christmas time.*

1 c. whole-wheat flour
1 c. all-purpose flour
1 c. oat bran
2 t. baking powder
2 t. baking soda
1 t. salt

2 eggs
3/4 c. brown sugar, packed
3/4 c. oil
1 c. milk
1 c. prepared mincemeat

In a large bowl, combine flours, bran, baking powder, baking soda
and salt. Mix well; make a well in the center and set aside. In a
separate small bowl, beat eggs; stir in brown sugar, oil, milk and
mincemeat. Pour egg mixture into flour mixture; stir just until
combined. Spoon batter into 18 to 24 greased muffin cups, filling each
2/3 full. Bake at 375 degrees for 20 minutes, or until muffins test
done with a toothpick. Makes 1-1/2 to 2 dozen.

Stack two cake stands together, smallest on top.
Cover with lemons, limes, hazelnuts and bundles of
fresh rosemary for a pretty two-tiered centerpiece.

Holiday Dinners
to Remember

Chicken & Dumplings

Gwendolyn Garren
Saluda, NC

This recipe was given to my mom by my grandmother. She cooked at a restaurant and this was always a favorite of customers. We all loved it too...I still make it often.

3-lb. whole chicken
2 c. self-rising flour

1/2 c. canola oil
salt and pepper to taste

Place chicken in a stockpot; cover with cold water. Bring to a boil over high heat. Reduce heat to medium-low. Cover and simmer for one to 1-1/2 hours, until chicken is very tender. Remove chicken to a plate. Reserve broth and strain; return 6 cups broth to stockpot and bring to a boil. In a large bowl, combine flour, oil and one to 1-1/2 cups of reserved hot broth; stir well to combine. Place half of dough on a floured surface. Roll out dough 1/4-inch thick; cut dough into 2-inch by one-inch strips. Repeat with remaining dough. Drop dumplings into boiling broth; stir to prevent sticking. Reduce heat to low; cook dumplings for 20 to 25 minutes. Shred or cut chicken into bite-size pieces; discard skin and bones. Add chicken to broth in stockpot; heat through. Season with salt and pepper. Serves 4.

Go ahead and unpack the Christmas tableware early in December...even the simplest meal is special when served on holly-trimmed plates!

Zesty Baked Chicken

Donna Scheletsky
Baden, PA

A family favorite! This recipe was given to me by a dear co-worker many years ago. We were always looking for yummy recipes to make after we came home from work.

1/4 c. butter, melted	1/4 t. salt
1/4 t. garlic powder	1/2 t. pepper
1/2 c. dry bread crumbs	1/4 t. paprika
1/4 c. grated Parmesan cheese	4 boneless, skinless chicken
1 t. dried oregano	breasts

Combine melted butter and garlic powder in a shallow bowl. Combine bread crumbs, cheese and seasonings in a separate shallow bowl. Dip each chicken breast into melted butter; coat well in bread crumb mixture. Place in a lightly greased 13"x9" baking pan. Cover and bake at 350 degrees for 45 minutes to one hour. Uncover; bake an additional 15 minutes, or until chicken juices run clear. Serves 4.

On Christmas Eve, my whole family would go to my grandparents' house for dinner. The excitement would build all day to see what Grandma had made for us. Presents could not be unwrapped until dinner was served, all the dishes were done and Grandpa said it was OK. My family got to open a special present that Santa had left at their house...our special nightgowns that Grandma had made for us. Oh, how I loved my new nightgown! I couldn't wait until I got home to put it on. We all still get new pajamas for Christmas Eve. I give my daughter her new PJ's at Grandma's, then we put them on to go home and get our picture taken. On Christmas Day, everyone goes to my dad's house for dinner in their new Christmas PJ's . I am so glad that I can carry this tradition on with my siblings and their children.

–Barbara Smith, Brockway, PA

Romanian Smothered Chicken

Michelle Powell
Valley, AL

My Mimi always made this for me on my trips home from college. It's one of the first dishes I learned to make for my family. I still serve it today, subbing Greek yogurt for some of the sour cream. Serve with a side of fresh green peas.

1/4 c. butter
3 lbs. boneless, skinless chicken
   breasts, cubed
2 T. all-purpose flour
1 T. onion, chopped
2 c. sour cream and/or plain
   Greek yogurt

salt and pepper to taste
1 c. sliced mushrooms
1 t. dried parsley
1 T. poppy seed
1 T. lemon juice
cooked egg noodles
Garnish: paprika

Melt butter in a large skillet over medium-high heat. Cook chicken on all sides until golden; remove chicken to a bowl. Stir flour into remaining pan juices. Add onion and sour cream and/or yogurt; simmer over low heat for 3 to 5 minutes. Season with salt and pepper. Add mushrooms; return chicken to skillet. Stir in parsley and poppy seed. Cover and simmer over low heat about 30 minutes, until chicken is tender, stirring occasionally. Remove from heat; stir in lemon juice. Serve chicken and sauce over hot egg noodles, garnished with a sprinkle of paprika. Makes 6 servings.

Silver bells...arrange votives in plain glass votive holders on a silver serving tray. Wind shiny silver beads between the votives with a scattering of silver jingle bells.

Roast Lemon-Pepper Chicken
Krista Marshall
Fort Wayne, IN

If you have a smaller family, or not everyone can make it home for the holiday, a large ham or turkey for Christmas dinner may be too much. This simple and delicious chicken is perfect!

2 T. olive oil
juice of 2 lemons, divided
7 to 8 chicken thighs
1-1/2 t. dried parsley

1 to 2 T. lemon-pepper
    seasoning
salt and pepper to taste

Place a wire rack on a large baking sheet. Spray rack and baking sheet with non-stick vegetable spray; set aside. In a small bowl, mix olive oil and half of the lemon juice. Brush chicken pieces with oil mixture on both sides; sprinkle with seasonings. Place chicken skin-side up on wire rack. Bake, uncovered, at 400 degrees for 30 minutes; reduce oven to 375 degrees. Bake for an additional 30 minutes, or until chicken juices run clear. Remove chicken to a serving platter; immediately drizzle with remaining lemon juice. Serves 4.

Nostalgic holiday postcards make charming placecards. Punch two holes in the top, string with thin velvet ribbon, tie on a pair of jingle bells and loop around dining room chair backs.

Noni's Baked Pork Chops

Eleanor Dionne
Beverly, MA

*My mom used to make this one-dish dinner when I was growing up.
With all the combined flavors, it smells so good when cooking...you
can't wait to eat! Now I make it for my own family. My sisters and
nieces make it for their families too.*

1 to 2 T. olive or canola oil
6 pork chops, 1-inch thick
3 cloves garlic, minced
2 onions, sliced
3 to 4 potatoes, peeled
    and quartered

salt and pepper to taste
24-oz. can pasta sauce
1/3 c. shredded Cheddar
    cheese

Coat a deep 13"x9" baking pan with oil. Layer pork chops, garlic,
onions and potatoes in pan. Season with salt and pepper. Pour pasta
sauce over top; sprinkle with cheese. Cover and bake at 375 degrees
for 1-1/2 hours. Uncover and bake for one additional hour. Makes
6 servings.

Bake up some sweet and tangy cranberry corn muffins
for dinner! Just stir dried cranberries and a little orange zest
into a cornbread muffin mix. Bake as directed on the package...
serve topped with a pat of butter.

108

Poppy's Italian Sausage & Potatoes *Kimberly Smith*
Shreveport, LA

This recipe was created by my Grandfather Poppy, who was old-school Italian. He would make it every Christmas along with his lasagna. He taught me how to make homemade croutons and that's the special touch I add.

5 to 7 russet potatoes, peeled, halved lengthwise and thinly sliced
3 sweet potatoes, peeled, halved lengthwise and thinly sliced
salt and pepper to taste
1/3 c. olive oil
6 sweet or hot Italian pork sausage links, each cut into 3 pieces

1 red onion, sliced and separated into rings
2 c. favorite-flavor croutons
Garnish: chopped fresh Italian parsley, grated Parmesan cheese

Arrange all potato slices in a lightly greased roasting pan. Sprinkle with salt and pepper; drizzle evenly with olive oil. Combine with your hands to make sure potatoes are evenly coated. Bake, uncovered, at 400 degrees for about one hour, until just barely fork-tender. Arrange sausage pieces over top. Reduce oven to 375 degrees; bake for 35 minutes. Arrange onion rings on top; continue to bake for 20 minutes. Sprinkle with croutons; continue baking for 15 minutes. Remove from oven; gently stir with a large slotted spoon until well combined. At serving time, sprinkle with parsley and Parmesan cheese. Makes 6 to 8 servings.

Quickly turn a group of mismatched tag-sale candleholders into a shimmering set...spray them all with the same color of craft paint.

Pork Chop Goulash

Marsha Lipomi
North Andover, MA

My aunt made this dish for me when I visited her in Texas years ago. I loved it then and I still love it now. My daughter makes it for her family too. Easy and delicious!

8-oz. pkg. wide egg noodles, uncooked
1 T. olive oil
1 onion, chopped

5 pork chops
2 10-3/4 oz. cans cream of mushroom soup

Cook noodles according to package directions; drain. Meanwhile, heat olive oil in a skillet over medium heat. Add onion to skillet; sauté for 2 minutes. Add pork chops; brown on both sides, about 5 minutes. Spoon soup over pork chops; reduce heat to low. Cover and simmer for 20 to 25 minutes, until bubbly and pork chops are cooked through. To serve, place cooked noodles on dinner plates; top with pork chops and sauce. Makes 5 servings.

Buttermilk Biscuits

Vickie

Serve these tender biscuits warm from the oven with creamy butter and homemade jam...yum!

2 c. all-purpose flour
1 t. baking soda
1 t. cream of tartar

1/8 t. salt
3 T. shortening
1 c. buttermilk

In a large bowl, mix flour, baking soda, cream of tartar and salt. Cut in shortening with a fork until fine crumbs form. Stir in buttermilk until a soft dough forms. On a floured surface, roll out dough 1/2-inch thick; cut with a biscuit cutter. Place biscuits on a greased baking sheet. Bake at 450 degrees for 10 to 12 minutes, until lightly golden. Makes one dozen.

Tuck a string of tiny white lights into a flower arrangement for extra sparkle.

Grandmother's Bacon Goulash

Lori Hill
Gretna, NE

Years ago, my grandmother went to make goulash and found she was out of ground beef. So she decided to substitute bacon...it has been a family favorite ever since. When I bring leftovers to work, everyone wants them! Be sure to cook the bacon very crisp as it softens in the tomato sauce.

2 lbs. thin-sliced bacon,
  chopped
16-oz. pkg. elbow macaroni,
  uncooked

4 15-oz. cans tomato sauce
2 T. sugar
salt and pepper to taste

In a large skillet over medium-high heat, cook bacon until very crisp; drain. Meanwhile, cook elbow macaroni according to package directions, just until tender. Drain; return cooked macaroni to cooking pot. Add crumbled bacon, tomato sauce and sugar to macaroni. Simmer over medium-low heat for 15 minutes, or until sauce thickens, stirring frequently. Season with salt and pepper. Makes 8 servings.

Get a head start on your holiday open house. Bundle up silverware in cloth napkins a few days in advance and then just place in a big basket...all ready to go to the table when you are!

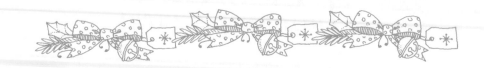

Slow-Cooker Chicken Olé

Diann Guy
Tulsa, OK

This is a very simple but tasty recipe that we came up with while attending college. Three other women and their husbands would come over and each would bring part of the ingredients. We students did not have a lot of money and we turned that evening into a wonderful adventure plus games and fellowship. Good with a tossed green salad and tangy French dressing.

10-3/4 oz. can cream of chicken soup
10-3/4 oz. can cream of celery soup
10-3/4 oz. can cream of mushroom soup
10-oz. can diced tomatoes with green chiles

1 onion, chopped
3-lb. deli roast chicken, shredded and divided
10-oz. pkg. shredded Colby Longhorn cheese, divided
7-oz. pkg. nacho cheese tortilla chips, crushed and divided

Mix soups, tomatoes and onion in a bowl. In a slow cooker, layer half each of chicken, soup mixture, cheese and chips. Repeat, ending with chips on top. Cover and cook on high setting for 2 to 3 hours, watching closely, until bubbly and heated through. Turn setting to low; may keep warm up to 3 hours. Makes 4 to 6 servings.

Love candlelight at Christmas, but you're concerned about children and pets knocking over lit candles? Tuck battery-operated tealights and pillars into favorite votives, sconces and centerpieces for a safe, soft glow.

Tangy Glazed Chicken

Vickie

Molasses gives this tender chicken old-fashioned flavor.

1/2 c. all-purpose flour
salt and pepper to taste
3 to 4 lbs. chicken, skinless
   if desired
1/2 c. oil
2/3 c. lemon juice

2/3 c. catsup
2/3 c. molasses
1/4 c. Worcestershire sauce
1 t. ground cloves
cooked rice

Combine flour, salt and pepper in a large plastic zipping bag. Add chicken, several pieces at a time; shake to coat and set aside. Heat oil in a large skillet over medium-high heat. Add chicken; cook for 10 minutes, or until golden, turning once. Drain chicken on paper towels. Drain skillet; wipe clean with paper towels. Return chicken to skillet. In a small bowl, combine remaining ingredients except rice; stir well and pour over chicken. Bring to a boil over medium-high heat. Reduce heat to medium-low. Cover and simmer for 35 to 40 minutes, until chicken juices run clear. Serve chicken over cooked rice, topped with some of the glaze from skillet. Serves 6.

A real conversation starter...ask older relatives about their earliest holiday memories. Did they have a Christmas tree? How was it decorated? Do they recall setting out cookies & milk for Santa? Don't miss the opportunity to preserve these precious memories on video!

Parmesan Chicken

Pieterina Hengstmengel
Picture Butte, Alberta

*I found this recipe a couple years ago, and it's now a family favorite.
I have had many people ask for the recipe. Try it and be amazed!*

1 c. butter, melted
1/4 c. mustard
1/8 t. salt
2 t. Worcestershire sauce

2 c. dry bread crumbs
1 c. grated Parmesan cheese
6 boneless, skinless chicken
  breasts

In a deep bowl, mix together melted butter, mustard, salt and Worcestershire sauce; set aside. Combine bread crumbs and cheese in a plastic zipping bag; shake until mixed thoroughly. Place in a separate deep bowl. Dip chicken into butter mixture, then into bread crumb mixture. Place chicken in a lightly greased 13"x9" glass baking pan. Bake, uncovered, at 350 degrees for 45 minutes, or until golden and chicken juices run clear, turning halfway through. Serves 6.

When I was very young, we went to Grandma and Grandpa's every Christmas Eve. We would stay until midnight waiting for Santa to come. We were too excited to nap, so we would run to the window every now and then. When the time came, we would hear a noise and take off outside to look. Sure enough, Santa had come...there were gifts on the porch and reindeer hoofprints in the snow! We were in heaven, not a lot of gifts but well worth the wait! I will always remember this from my childhood.

–Elizabeth Smithson, Cunningham, KY

Baked Dijonnaise Chicken

Paula Marchesi
Lenhartsville, PA

I came up with this dish one night when I was in a hurry and didn't know what to fix. Everyone loved it! Now my family requests this quite often. Enjoy!

1/2 c. Dijonnaise-style creamy
  Dijon mustard
1/3 c. brown sugar, packed
1/2 t. cinnamon

1/8 t. cayenne pepper
8 boneless, skinless chicken
  thighs

In a large bowl, mix mustard, brown sugar and spices. Reserve 1/4 cup of mixture to serve with cooked chicken. Add chicken to remaining mixture; toss to coat. Arrange chicken in a 13"x9" baking pan sprayed with non-stick vegetable spray. Bake, uncovered, at 350 degrees for 35 to 45 minutes, until chicken juices run clear. Serve chicken with reserved mustard mixture. Makes 8 servings.

Wrapped in love! Use children's drawings as wrapping paper for holiday gifts. Perfect for doting grandparents and aunts & uncles.

Christmas Ravioli Bake

Amy Hunt
Traphill, NC

This dish is layered with Christmas colors and is a quick-fix meal for the busy holiday season. Just add a crisp salad and cheesy biscuits... don't forget dessert! It's easily doubled for entertaining.

32-oz. jar spaghetti sauce,
  divided
20-oz. pkg. refrigerated
  meat-filled ravioli, divided
1 t. garlic salt

10-oz. pkg. frozen spinach,
  thawed and squeezed dry
2 c. shredded Mozzarella
  cheese, divided
1/4 c. grated Parmesan cheese

Spray an 8"x8" baking pan with non-stick vegetable spray. Spoon 1/4 cup spaghetti sauce over bottom of pan. Layer with half of the ravioli; spread half of remaining sauce over ravioli and sprinkle with garlic salt. Add spinach; sprinkle with half of the mozzarella cheese. Repeat layering with ravioli, sauce and mozzarella cheese; sprinkle with Parmesan cheese. Cover pan with aluminum foil. Bake at 375 degrees for 30 minutes. Remove foil; bake for an additional 10 minutes. Serves 4.

Set up a mini Christmas tree in the kids' rooms...a great way for them to show off homemade and favorite ornaments of their very own.

Melt-in-Your-Mouth
Country-Style Steak

Jessica Hawks
Fort Campbell, KY

My mother-in-law introduced this recipe to me nearly 20 years ago.
My husband has always loved it...it quickly became a favorite
of mine too. Definitely melts in your mouth!

1 c. oil
1 c. all-purpose flour
1/2 t. sea salt
1/2 t. pepper
1 t. garlic powder
1-1/2 lbs. beef cube steak

1/2 c. green pepper, finely
   chopped
2-1/2 c. milk
cooked rice, egg noodles or
   mashed potatoes

Heat oil in a Dutch oven over medium heat. While oil is heating, combine flour and seasonings in a shallow dish. Lightly coat beef with flour mixture. Add beef to hot oil; cook on both sides until browned and a crust begins to form. Add green pepper, milk and remaining flour mixture; stir lightly until all ingredients are coated. Reduce heat to low. Cover and simmer for 40 to 45 minutes, until beef is very tender. Serve beef and gravy from skillet over cooked rice, egg noodles or mashed potatoes. Serves 5.

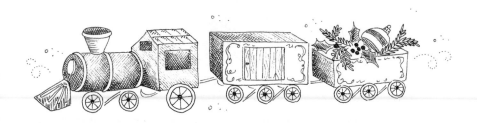

Revive a childhood tradition...add an old-fashioned
toy train (complete with a whistle!) under
the tree this year.

Nana's Mostaccioli

Lynn Rogers
Saint Johns, FL

My mom was a good cook and cooked wonderful meals for our family. At the time we didn't know they were inexpensive too... we just knew how good they tasted.

16-oz. pkg. mostaccioli pasta, uncooked
6 slices bacon
1 lb. ground beef

2 onions, chopped
2 10-3/4 oz. cans tomato soup
1-1/2 c. shredded Cheddar cheese

Cook pasta according to package directions; drain and place in a large bowl. Meanwhile, in a large skillet over medium heat, cook bacon until crisp. Remove bacon to a separate bowl, reserving drippings in skillet. Add beef and onions to drippings; cook until beef is no longer pink. Stir in soup; heat through. Ladle beef mixture over pasta and toss to coat. Transfer to a lightly greased 13"x9" baking pan; top with crumbled bacon. Bake, uncovered, at 350 degrees for 45 minutes. Top with cheese; bake for an additional 15 minutes, or until cheese is melted. Makes 8 servings.

For a quick-as-a-wink table runner, lay wide ribbon across the table's length and width.

Granddaddy's Meatloaf

Beverley Williams
San Antonio, TX

This was my granddaddy's recipe. He served it in the restaurant he owned in the 1920s and continued to make it for family dinners as I was growing up. It is one of the first things he taught me to cook.

2 lbs. ground beef
1 lb. ground pork breakfast
   sausage
2 c. mashed potatoes

1 yellow onion, finely chopped
1 t. pepper
1/2 c. catsup

In a large bowl, combine all ingredients except catsup; mix well. Add catsup, a little at a time, until mixture is moistened. Form mixture into a loaf; place in an ungreased 9"x5" loaf pan. Bake, uncovered, at 350 degrees for one hour, or until no longer pink in the center. Cool slightly before slicing. Serves 8.

I truly believe that if we keep telling the Christmas story, singing the Christmas songs, and living the Christmas spirit, we can bring joy and happiness and peace to this world.

–Norman Vincent Peale

Beef Paprika

Jill VanLandingham
Pittsburgh, PA

This recipe is one of my favorite meals and I often choose it for my birthday dinner. The flavor is mild and warm, always a great winter treat. Even family members who don't care for onion in recipes will eat this by the plateful!

2 to 3 T. oil
1/2 c. all-purpose flour
salt and pepper to taste
3-lb. beef rump roast, cut into
   1-inch cubes
4 sweet onions, chopped
6-oz. can tomato paste

2 c. water
2 T. paprika, or to taste
6 to 8 servings long-cooking
   brown or white rice,
   uncooked
1 to 2 c. frozen peas, thawed

Drizzle oil into a large slow cooker; preheat on high setting. Combine flour, salt and pepper in a large plastic zipping bag. Add beef cubes; shake to coat well and add to slow cooker. Cook, stirring occasionally, until lightly browned. Add onions to slow cooker. Cook for 4 to 5 minutes, until almost translucent, stirring occasionally. Stir in tomato paste, water and paprika. Cover and cook on low setting for 6 to 8 hours, stirring once or twice if desired. About 40 minutes before serving time, cook rice according to package directions. Stir peas into cooked rice. Serve beef mixture ladled over rice mixture. Serves 6 to 8.

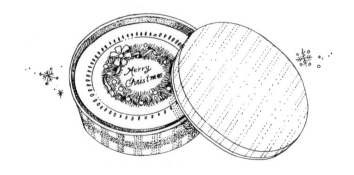

Don't wait until Christmas Day to use your festive holiday dishes...use them all season long for a daily dose of cheer!

Holiday Dinners
to Remember

Kathleen's Dill Pickle Pot Roast   *Kathleen Walker*
Mountain Center, CA

*Trust me, it tastes great! This recipe is a favorite with our family.
My firefighter son Tim always asks for it when he visits.*

2 to 3 T. oil
3 to 4-lb. beef chuck roast
3/4 c. all-purpose flour
8-oz. pkg. sliced mushrooms
3 small whole dill pickles,
   chopped

1 onion, chopped
1/2 c. beef broth
1 bay leaf
8-oz. container sour cream
salt and pepper to taste

Heat oil in a heavy skillet over medium heat. Coat roast with flour;
brown on all sides in oil. Drain; remove roast to an ungreased roasting
pan. Combine mushrooms, pickles, onion and broth in a bowl; spoon
over roast. Tuck bay leaf into pan. Cover and bake at 325 degrees for
2 hours. During the last 30 minutes, uncover pan if roast seems too
juicy. Remove roast to a serving platter; let stand for several minutes
before slicing. Discard bay leaf. Stir sour cream into pan juices; season
with salt and pepper. Serve sour cream gravy with sliced beef. Serves
10 to 12.

Start a new tradition...hide a glass pickle ornament
among the branches of a decorated tree. When it's time
to pack away the decorations, whoever finds the
pickle gets a small prize!

Slow-Cooker Ham & Beans

Renae Scheiderer
Beallsville, OH

This is my go-to recipe in fall and winter. We have a dairy farm and I also work at our local diner, and this is so easy to put together. It's wonderful to come home to a delicious dinner all ready & waiting! Serve with cornbread.

16-oz. pkg. dried Great
   Northern beans
2 t. onion powder

salt and pepper to taste
6 c. water
1 lb. ham bone, hocks or shanks

In a large slow cooker, combine dried beans, seasonings and water; add ham. Cover and cook on low setting for 8 hours, or until beans are tender. Cut the meat from ham bone; discard bone. Return meat to slow cooker and mix into beans. Makes 10 to 12 servings.

Invite friends to join you for a favorite skillet or slow-cooker supper in December...a meal shared with friends doesn't need to be fancy. After all, it's friendship that makes it special!

Tender Pork Loin & Kraut

Tina Hanks
Wilmington, OH

*I enjoy making this tummy-warming dish in the slow cooker
for my family in wintertime. It makes for a very tasty and
easy supper. Mashed potatoes go very well with this.*

3 to 5-lb. boneless pork loin
1/2 c. Worcestershire sauce
3/4 c. brown sugar, packed and
  divided

1 to 2 32-oz. jars sauerkraut,
  drained

Place pork loin in a glass or plastic container; coat generously with
Worcestershire sauce. Cover and refrigerate for 2 hours to overnight;
drain. Place pork loin in a slow cooker; spread 1/4 cup brown sugar
over top. Cover and cook on high setting for 2 hours. Add sauerkraut;
top with remaining brown sugar. Cover and cook on high setting
another 2 to 3 hours, until tender. Serves 8 to 12.

Eunice's Red Cinnamon Apples

Carrie Fostor
Baltic, OH

*I remember my Grandma Hobart making these sweet apples
for holidays. She received the recipe from her Aunt Eunice.*

6 Jonathan apples, peeled,
  halved and cored
1 c. sugar
1/2 c. red cinnamon candies

1/2 c. water
Optional: 1 to 2 drops red food
  coloring

In a large bowl, cover apples with cold water; let stand. Meanwhile,
combine sugar, candies and water in a large saucepan over medium
heat. Cook and stir until sugar and candies are dissolved. Stir in food
coloring, if desired. Drain apples; add to sugar syrup. Cook until
apples are fork-tender, turning often. Remove apples to a platter;
spoon some of the syrup over them. May be made ahead, covered
and refrigerated for several days. Makes 12 servings.

Italian Sausage in Beer

Annette Ceravolo
Hoover, AL

I like to use both mild and hot sausage for this recipe, but if you're really brave, use only hot sausage. Either way, it's easy and delicious. It is also good as an appetizer.

1 lb. mild Italian pork sausage
    link, cut into 1/2-inch pieces
1 lb. hot Italian pork sausage
    link, cut into 1/2-inch pieces
1 onion, minced

1 c. regular or non-alcoholic
    beer
1/2 t. hot pepper sauce
Optional: 1 T. fresh parsley,
    finely chopped

In a deep skillet over medium-high heat, cook sausage for 5 to 7 minutes, until lightly golden. Drain, if needed. Add onion; cook for 5 to 6 minutes. Reduce heat to low. Stir in beer, hot sauce and parsley, if using. Simmer for 10 to 12 minutes, stirring every 3 to 4 minutes. Remove from heat. Transfer to a chafing dish or serving bowl. Freezes well for future use. Makes 8 to 10 servings.

December is jam-packed with baking, shopping and decorating, so take it easy with simple, hearty meals. Make double batches of family favorites like chili or Sloppy Joes early in the holiday season. Freeze half to heat & eat later. You'll be so glad you did!

Smoky Green Beans & Taters

Stephanie Simms
Lafayette, IN

*This slow-cooker recipe is one of our favorite
stick-to-your-ribs meals when it is cold outside.*

2 14-1/2 oz. cans green beans
4 14-1/2 oz. cans whole new
   potatoes, drained
salt and pepper to taste
1 lb. smoked pork sausage link,
   sliced

2 10-3/4 oz. cans cream of
   mushroom soup
1 c. shredded Cheddar cheese

Pour green beans with liquid into a large slow cooker. Layer potatoes
over beans; season with salt and pepper. Add sausage; top with soup
and cheese. Cover and cook on low setting for 4 to 6 hours. Stir before
serving. Makes 8 servings.

Make herbed butter in a jiffy...scrumptious on warm bread or
melting into mashed potatoes. Unwrap a stick of butter and
cut it in half lengthwise. Roll each half in finely chopped fresh
parsley, rosemary, chives and thyme, then slice and serve.

Mom's One-Pot Chicken Supper

Shirley Howie
Foxboro, MA

My mother made this easy and delicious old standby so many times when we were kids. Recently I found it when I was going through her recipe collection...now I am making it for my hubby and me!

2 T. butter, sliced
2 lbs. chicken
1 clove garlic, minced
10-3/4 oz. can tomato soup
10-1/2 oz. can beef broth
1-1/4 c. water

1 t. dried oregano
Optional: 1/2 t. salt
1/8 t. pepper
1 c. long-cooking rice, uncooked
10-oz. pkg. frozen peas

Melt butter in a large skillet over medium heat. Add chicken pieces and garlic; cook until chicken is golden on both sides. In a bowl, combine soup, broth, water and seasonings; spoon over chicken in skillet. Reduce heat to low. Cover and simmer for 20 minutes. Stir in uncooked rice and peas. Cover and cook an additional 25 minutes, or until chicken juices run clear and rice is tender, stirring occasionally. Serves 4.

Be prepared for a winter's snowstorm! Stock your pantry with canned vegetables, creamy soups, rice mixes, pasta and other handy meal-makers.

Cozy Chicken & Noodles

Kathy Kyler
Norman, OK

I got this slow-cooker recipe from a co-worker several years ago. It is my husband's favorite meal in cold weather, and it reheats well. Serve with some crusty bread to mop up the tasty sauce...it will chase away the winter chills!

10-3/4 oz. can cream of
   chicken soup
4 c. chicken broth
3 carrots, peeled and chopped
3 stalks celery, chopped
1/4 c. butter, sliced
1 t. garlic powder

pepper to taste
1 bay leaf
4 boneless, skinless chicken
   breasts
8-oz. pkg. wide egg noodles,
   uncooked

In a slow cooker, stir together soup, broth, vegetables, butter and seasonings. Push chicken down into mixture. Cover and cook on low setting for 6 to 8 hours. About 30 minutes before serving, turn slow cooker to high setting. Stir uncooked noodles into mixture in slow cooker. Cover and cook until noodles are tender, 10 to 15 minutes. At serving time, discard bay leaf. Remove chicken; cool slightly and shred, then stir back into noodle mixture. To serve, ladle into bowls. Makes 8 servings.

Fill up the slow cooker with a hearty dinner in the morning.
After supper, you'll be able to get an early start on a cozy family
evening, watching a favorite holiday movie together.

Great-Grandma's Chicken Tetrazzini

Marci Watts
Mount Prospect, IL

This recipe comes from my great-grandmother and was passed on to me by my mom. It is easy and tastes wonderful...just add a crisp salad and hot rolls for a quick holiday meal.

1-1/4 to 1-1/2 c. spaghetti, uncooked and broken up
1-1/2 to 2 c. cooked chicken, cubed
1/4 c. green pepper, chopped
1/4 c. onion, chopped
1/4 c. canned diced pimentos, drained
10-3/4 oz. can cream of mushroom soup
1/2 c. chicken broth or water
Optional: 1 T. sherry
1/2 t. salt
1/8 t. pepper
8-oz. pkg. shredded Cheddar cheese, divided

Cook spaghetti according to package directions; drain. Combine cooked spaghetti, chicken and vegetables in a large bowl; mix gently. Stir in soup, broth or water and sherry, if using. Season with salt and pepper. Fold in 1-1/4 cups cheese. Toss together lightly with 2 forks. Transfer mixture to a greased 1-1/2 quart casserole dish. Sprinkle with remaining cheese. Bake at 350 degrees for 45 minutes, or until hot and bubbly. Casserole may also be covered and frozen, unbaked. To serve, thaw in the refrigerator; bake as directed. Makes 4 to 6 servings.

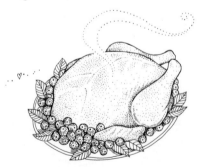

Choosing a turkey for the holiday? Allow about one pound per person plus a little extra for leftovers. For example, a 15-pound turkey would serve 12 people with enough left to enjoy turkey sandwiches, turkey tetrazzini or turkey soup afterwards.

Debby's Chicken Lasagna

Debby Conaway
Rome, GA

This delicious recipe takes just four hours...pretty fast for a slow-cooker recipe. It's great when the holidays are hectic and you are in a pinch for time. Feel free to double the recipe if your slow cooker is large enough.

3 boneless, skinless chicken
    breasts, cooked and
    shredded
26-oz. jar spaghetti sauce
9-oz. pkg. lasagna noodles,
    uncooked and divided

1 c. ricotta cheese, divided
1 c. shredded mozzarella cheese,
    divided
1 c. shredded Cheddar cheese

In a bowl, mix chicken with sauce. Layer in an oval slow cooker as follows: 1/3 of chicken mixture, 1/3 of uncooked noodles, 1/3 of ricotta cheese and 1/3 of mozzarella cheese. Break noodles to fit as they are added. Repeat layering twice; top with Cheddar cheese. Cover and cook on high setting for 3 hours. Turn setting to low; continue cooking for one hour, or until bubbly and noodles are tender. Makes 8 servings.

Make spirits bright by stitching pompoms onto plain winter hats, scarves and mittens. Super-easy to do with just a needle and thread!

Turkey Tourtière

Susan Black
Campbell River, British Columbia

This savory meat pie is a Christmas tradition in Canada. As family members got older, though, using pork as the main ingredient didn't sit well with our digestive systems. I switched out the pork for turkey and it worked beautifully. Use your own homemade pie crusts or convenient ready-made crusts.

1-1/2 to 2 lbs. ground turkey
1 clove garlic, pressed
1 onion, chopped
1/2 c. hot water
1/4 t. celery salt

1/4 t. ground cloves
salt and pepper to taste
Optional: 1/4 c. dry bread
   crumbs
2 9-inch pie crusts

In a large saucepan, combine turkey, garlic, onion, hot water and seasonings. Cook over low heat for 20 to 25 minutes; remove from heat and let cool. If desired, stir in bread crumbs. Arrange one pie crust in a 9-inch pie plate. Spoon in turkey filling; cover with top crust. Pinch edges together to seal crust; cut several slits with a knife tip. Bake at 350 degrees for about 35 minutes, until bubbly and crust is golden. Cut into wedges. Makes 6 servings.

Before adding the top crust to a pie, cut out vents with a mini cookie cutter...little hearts and stars leave the prettiest patterns!

Holiday Dinners to Remember

Turkey Shortcakes

Laura Fuller
Fort Wayne, IN

After Thanksgiving and Christmas, my family was getting pretty bored with turkey leftovers. This dish is similar to a pot pie...we all really enjoy it! Good over cooked rice too.

1 T. butter
1/2 c. onion, chopped
3/4 c. baby carrots, thinly sliced
2 stalks celery, thinly sliced
1/4 c. sliced mushrooms
1-1/2 c. turkey or chicken broth
1/2 t. salt
1/4 t. pepper

1/2 c. milk
2 T. all-purpose flour
2 c. cooked turkey, cubed
1 c. frozen baby peas
1/3 c. fresh dill, snipped
4 jumbo buttermilk biscuits,
    baked and split

Melt butter in a saucepan over medium heat. Add onion; cook until tender, about 5 minutes. Increase heat to medium-high. Add carrots, celery, mushrooms, broth, salt and pepper; bring to a boil. Reduce heat to low. Simmer for 10 to 12 minutes, until vegetables are tender. Meanwhile, shake together milk and flour in a small covered jar until blended. Whisking constantly, pour milk mixture into hot mixture in pan. Bring to a boil; boil for one minute, or until thickened. Stir in turkey, peas and dill; heat through. To serve, spoon turkey mixture over biscuit halves. Makes 4 servings.

A centerpiece that's ready in an instant! Fill clear glass hurricanes with bright red and green shiny Christmas balls to decorate your holiday dinner table.

Sour Cream Beef

Maile Helekahi
Honolulu, HI

I can remember my Uncle Isao making this for dinner when I was a kid. Now that I have my own kitchen, I make this dish at least twice a month because I love the sauce! Every time I cook this, I can see his smiling face. My Aunty Lily shared her variation with me...adding a splash of vermouth. Though I haven't tried it yet, feel free to.

1 c. butter, sliced
1-1/2 lb. beef round steak,
   thinly sliced
8-oz. pkg. sliced mushrooms
1 onion, sliced
10-3/4 oz. can tomato soup

6-oz. can tomato paste
1 t. Worcestershire sauce
1 t. salt
pepper to taste
8-oz. container sour cream
cooked rice

Melt butter in a large skillet over medium heat. Add beef and mushrooms; cook until browned on all sides. Add onion; cook until softened. In a bowl, combine soup, tomato paste, Worcestershire sauce, salt and pepper. Add soup mixture to beef mixture. Reduce heat to low. Cover and simmer for one hour, stirring occasionally. Stir in sour cream during last 10 minutes. To serve, ladle beef mixture over cooked rice. Makes 4 to 6 servings.

Make a trivet in a jiffy to protect the tabletop from hot dishes. Simply attach a cork or felt square to the bottom of a large ceramic tile with craft glue. It's so easy, why not make a few extra to give as gifts?

Martha's Green-Chiladas

Bunny Palmertree
Carrollton, MS

My sister-in-law Martha shared this recipe with me many years ago.
It's delicious and easy...requested at all family get-togethers.

1-1/2 lbs. ground beef
1/4 c. onion, chopped
10-3/4 oz. can cream of
   mushroom soup
1-1/4 c. milk
4-oz. can chopped green chiles

10-oz. pkg. regular or spicy
   nacho cheese tortilla chips,
   crushed and divided
2 c. shredded Cheddar cheese,
   divided

In a large skillet over medium heat, brown beef with onion; drain.
Meanwhile, mix soup with milk in a bowl. Stir in undrained chiles and
set aside. In a 13"x9" baking pan coated with non-stick vegetable
spray, layer half the tortilla chips, half the beef mixture and half the
cheese. Repeat layers; spoon soup mixture over top. Bake, uncovered,
at 350 degrees for 45 minutes, or until hot and bubbly. Makes
8 servings.

Christmas decorations don't have to be all pine and holly!
For a quick and casual centerpiece, curl a string of dried
chile peppers into a circle, then set a hurricane with
a fat red candle in the center.

Wheelerwood Church Casserole

Helen Thoen
Manly, IA

During World War II when rubber was rationed, my parents preserved the tires on their car by attending nearby Wheelerwood Community Church, rather than driving to the church where they were members. When this dish was served at a church potluck, it was such a big hit that many ladies wanted the recipe. This recipe comes from my mom's recipe box, on the scrap of paper she wrote it on that day. Mom made it often and it really is delicious.

8-oz. pkg. wide egg noodles, uncooked
1 lb. ground beef
salt and pepper to taste
2 c. celery, sliced
1 c. onion, chopped
1 green pepper, chopped
1 to 2 T. oil
2 14-1/2 oz. cans diced tomatoes

Cook noodles according to package directions, just until tender. Drain noodles; transfer to a lightly greased 3-quart casserole dish. Meanwhile, in a skillet over medium heat, brown beef until no longer pink; drain. Season beef with salt and pepper; add to noodles. In same skillet, sauté celery, onion and green pepper in oil until tender; drain. Add celery mixture and tomatoes with juice to noodle mixture; stir gently. Cover and bake at 350 degrees for 45 minutes. Makes 5 to 6 servings.

Pick up some paintable wooden cut-outs in holiday shapes at a neighborhood craft store. They're fun and easy for kids to decorate as package tie-ons that can later be used as tree ornaments.

Red Gravy Pot Roast

Judy Couto
Kerman, CA

This slow-cooker recipe was given to me years ago by a very dear friend. Her grandma used to serve it at her boarding house many, many years ago. I started making it when the kids were young...at the time, I was low on money and it went far. It has become a family favorite, so good for Sunday dinner after church! Be sure to use the catsup with "57 Varieties" on the label for delicious gravy.

1/4 c. plus 1 t. all-purpose flour
1/2 c. water
2 to 4-lb. beef rump roast
salt and pepper to taste

1 onion, thinly sliced
7-oz. bottle catsup
mashed potatoes

In a bowl, combine flour and enough water to make a thick paste. Spread paste over all sides of roast. Season roast well with salt and pepper; place in a slow cooker. Cover roast with onion slices; add all of the catsup. Add enough water to cover roast halfway. Cover and cook 6 to 8 hours. Remove roast to a serving platter; let stand several minutes before slicing. Serve sliced roast over mashed potatoes, topped with gravy from the slow cooker. Makes 4 to 6 servings.

If you're traveling to join family for Christmas, make a trip bag for each of the kids...a special tote bag or backpack that's filled with favorite small toys, puzzles and other fun stuff, reserved just for road trips. The miles will speed by much faster!

Auntie Dee's Spaghetti Casserole

Debbie Muer
Encino, CA

My aunt used to make this easy spaghetti dish. It's really good!

16-oz. pkg. spaghetti or angel
    hair pasta, uncooked
1 to 2 lbs. ground beef
32-oz. jar spaghetti sauce

8-oz. container ricotta cheese
1 c. grated Parmesan cheese
16-oz. pkg. shredded
    mozzarella cheese, divided

Cook pasta according to package directions, just until tender; drain
and set aside. Meanwhile, brown beef in a large skillet over medium
heat; drain. In a large bowl, blend spaghetti sauce and ricotta cheese;
stir in beef, Parmesan cheese and 2 cups mozzarella cheese. Add
cooked pasta; stir gently to coat. Transfer mixture to a greased 3-quart
casserole dish; top with remaining cheese. Bake, uncovered, at
400 degrees for 30 minutes, or until bubbly and cheese is melted.
Makes 4 to 6 servings.

Collect pine cones to make a treat for the birds. Tie a
hanging string to the top of each pine cone, then spread
with peanut butter mixed with cornmeal and roll in
bird seed. The birds will love it!

136

Aunt Ruby's Noodle Casserole

Lynda Bolton
East Peoria, IL

When I stayed overnight with my favorite aunt and cousin, this is what we would have for supper. Once I had a family of my own, it became their favorite casserole too. We always think of my sweet aunt whenever I prepare it.

12-oz. pkg. wide egg noodles, uncooked
1 lb. lean ground beef or turkey
1/2 c. onion, chopped
2 10-3/4 oz. cans cream of mushroom, celery or chicken soup

15-oz. can corn, drained
8-oz. can sliced mushrooms, drained
6 slices American cheese

Cook noodles according to package directions, just until tender; drain. Meanwhile, in a large skillet over medium heat, cook meat and onion until browned; drain well. Add soup and cooked noodles to mixture in skillet; mix well. Spread in a 3-quart casserole dish sprayed with non-stick vegetable spray. Pour corn over top; gently press down. Spread mushrooms over corn; arrange cheese slices over the top of casserole. Bake, uncovered, at 350 degrees for 45 minutes, or until hot, bubbly and cheese is melted. Makes 6 to 8 servings.

As winter evenings turn dark, light a candle or two at the family dinner table. It'll make an ordinary meal seem special!

137

Fruited Cranberry Pork Roast

Dottie Russo
Springfield, PA

This recipe came from a dear friend who's a fabulous cook! We we live next door to each other and started our friendship over the picket fence. The two of us have been friends for the past 23 years and still exchange recipes and entertaining ideas. I double this recipe because it is so, so good. Delicious with mashed potatoes.

3-lb. boneless pork loin	1 t. dry mustard
15-oz. can jellied cranberry sauce	1/4 t. ground cloves
	2 T. cornstarch
1/2 c. sugar	2 T. cold water
1/2 c. cranberry or apple juice	

Place pork loin in a slow cooker; set aside. In a bowl, combine cranberry sauce, sugar, fruit juice, mustard and cloves. Mix well, breaking up cranberry sauce as much as possible. Spoon mixture over pork. Cover and cook on low setting for 7 to 8 hours. Remove pork loin to a serving platter; cover to keep warm. Combine cornstarch and cold water in a small jar; cover and shake until dissolved. Pour mixture into juices in slow cooker; stir well. Turn slow cooker to high setting; cover and cook for about 15 minutes, until thickened. To serve, drizzle sliced pork with sauce. Serve remaining sauce on the side in a gravy boat. Makes 4 to 5 servings.

Fresh red roses or carnations make a delightfully different winter centerpiece. Arrange in a big vase with glossy green holly or delicate ferns.

Holiday Dinners
to Remember

Slow-Cooked Paprika Ham

Linda Payne
Snow Hill, MD

A great holiday recipe! Put it together the night before, then pop it in the slow cooker in the morning. Almost no work!

1 c. paprika
3-1/2 T. brown sugar, packed

1/2 t. onion powder
8 to 10-lb. bone-in ham

Mix together paprika, brown sugar and onion powder in a bowl; rub over all sides of ham. Cover and refrigerate for 8 hours to overnight. Place ham in a large slow cooker. Cover and cook on low setting for 3 to 4 hours. Remove ham to a serving platter; let stand for 15 minutes before carving. Serves 12 to 15.

Mama's Baked Brown Sugar Ham

Connie Griffis
Macclenny, FL

Our special-occasion ham! This glazed ham is fork-tender, moist and delicious...the drippings are perfect on sweet potatoes.

2 c. brown sugar, packed and divided

10 to 12-lb. ham butt end

Rub one cup brown sugar over all sides of ham, using more brown sugar as necessary. Line a roasting pan with aluminum foil; cover inside of lid with foil. Sprinkle remaining brown sugar into pan; place ham in pan. Cover and bake at 350 degrees for 3-1/2 hours. Turn off oven. Leave ham while oven cools, about one hour. Remove ham to a serving platter; slice and serve. Makes 15 to 18 servings.

Don't toss out that dab of leftover cranberry sauce! Purée it with balsamic vinaigrette to create a tangy salad dressing.

Mom's Salmon Patties

Darcy Anders
Hendersonville, NC

For as long as I can remember, my grandmother and mother made these salmon patties for our family. They were always a favorite of mine as a child. They are now my daughter's favorite too...like mother, like daughter!

15-oz. can red salmon, drained
   and liquid reserved
1 egg, lightly beaten
2 T. all-purpose flour
2 T. onion, finely chopped
2 T. lemon juice

1 t. Worcestershire sauce
1/4 t. fresh parsley, chopped
1/2 c. potato chips, crushed
1 to 2 T. oil
Garnish: lemon wedges

Place salmon in a bowl; flake with a fork. Add egg, flour, onion, lemon juice, Worcestershire sauce, parsley, crushed potato chips and enough of reserved salmon liquid to moisten. Mix with fork until blended. Add more crushed chips if mixture becomes too moist. Form into 4 flattened patties. Heat oil in a skillet over medium heat. Add patties and cook until golden on both sides. Serve with lemon wedges. Makes 4 servings.

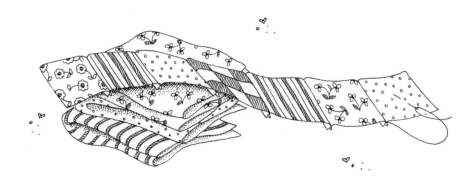

A gift Mom or Grandma is sure to love! A simple lap quilt is a sweet way to preserve the memories in children's outgrown clothing. Cut large squares and stitch together, then layer with thin batting and a fabric backing.

Holiday Dinners
to Remember

Honey-Mustard Roasted Salmon

Ann Heavey
Bridgewater, MA

This salmon comes out perfectly every time...it's easy, healthy and delicious! To change things up, I have added fresh rosemary or dill to the mustard mixture. Serve with lemon wedges, if you like.

1-lb. salmon fillet, about
   1-inch thick
3 T. spicy Dijon mustard

1-1/2 T. honey
1 t. olive oil
salt and pepper to taste

Spray a baking sheet lightly with non-stick vegetable spray. Place salmon skin-side down on baking sheet; set aside. Mix together mustard, honey and olive oil in a bowl; spread over top of salmon. Season with salt and pepper. Bake, uncovered, at 400 degrees for 18 to 20 minutes, until salmon flakes easily with a fork. Serves 4.

We are a big Italian family with many cherished traditions and my mother always kept true to the Christmas Eve Feast of the Seven Fishes. Over the years, my sisters and I got used to the tastes and smells that Christmas Eve brought with it. The strong fishy odor meant that Santa was near! When all of us got married, things were not that simple. My sisters and I brought to the family sons-in-law and grandchildren who were not so thrilled about our holiday feast. Some were not seafood fans while others claimed they were allergic. My mother quickly found a solution to excite her new family members about Christmas Eve at Nonnie's house. She has now added a fish-shaped meatloaf to our Christmas Eve traditions!

–Toni Oustrich, Taylor, PA

Alice's Simple Baked Shrimp *JoAlice Patterson-Welton*
Lawrenceville, GA

My mom was a home economics teacher and a great southern cook. This recipe was a family favorite, especially when we were at the beach in Florida and had access to fresh shrimp from the many shrimp boats nearby. It's wonderful served with tossed salad and garlic bread, or serve over pasta or rice, with some of the butter mixture drizzled on top.

1/2 c. butter, sliced
1 lemon, thinly sliced
1-1/2 to 2 lbs. uncooked
   shrimp, peeled and cleaned

1-oz. pkg. Italian salad dressing
   mix

Line a baking sheet and its sides with heavy-duty aluminum foil. Add butter to baking sheet; melt in a 350-degree oven. Place lemon slices over the melted butter; arrange shrimp over lemon. Sprinkle shrimp with salad dressing mix. Bake at 350 degrees for 15 minutes, or until lightly golden. Serves 4 to 6.

Share the holiday spirit with a good winter deed! Shovel the driveway and sidewalk for a neighbor.

Shrimp Portuguese

Cynthia Knight
North Attleboro, MA

I first tasted a version of this spicy dish on Christmas Eve at my husband's Portuguese uncle's home. It was so unusual and so flavorful that I had to try and make it. Uncle Agostinho gave me the basic ingredients, and I tested amounts until it was the perfect blend.

6 carrots, peeled and coarsely
   chopped
24-oz. jar tomato basil pasta
   sauce
1 c. white wine or chicken broth
1 t. cayenne pepper, or to taste
salt and pepper to taste

1 lb. uncooked fresh or frozen
   shrimp, thawed if frozen,
   peeled and cleaned
1/2 c. fresh flat-leaf parsley,
   chopped
Garnish: fresh basil

In a Dutch oven over medium-high heat, cover carrots with lightly salted water. Bring to a boil; boil until fork-tender. Drain; add pasta sauce to carrots. Finely mash carrots to blend with sauce. Add wine or broth, cayenne pepper, salt and pepper. Reduce heat to medium-low; simmer for 10 minutes. Meanwhile, prepare Garlic Bread. Add shrimp to sauce mixture. Simmer until pink, about 3 to 5 minutes; stir in parsley. To serve, place a slice of Garlic Bread in each shallow bowl. Ladle sauce and shrimp over bread. Garnish with basil; serve immediately. Serves 4 to 6.

Garlic Bread:

3 T. butter, sliced
3 cloves garlic, pressed

6 slices Portuguese or Italian
   bread, cut 1-inch thick

Melt butter in a small saucepan over medium heat. Add garlic; stir just until garlic begins to turn golden. Generously brush butter mixture over both sides of bread. Grill bread until lightly golden on both sides.

Tony's Tuna Hotdish

Carol Mick
Royalton, MN

This is what my family wants for Christmas every single year. It's always been my son Tony's favorite. We have the ham, potatoes, veggies, desserts...but it isn't Christmas without the Tuna Hotdish!

16-oz. pkg. wide egg noodles or
   rotini pasta, uncooked
4 c. celery, finely chopped
4 c. onions, chopped
26-oz. can cream of mushroom
   soup

1-1/2 c. milk
5 5-oz. cans tuna packed in
   water, well drained
salt and pepper to taste
6-oz. pkg. potato chips, crushed

Cook noodles or pasta according to package directions, adding celery and onions to the cooking water. Drain well; transfer to a large bowl. Add soup, milk, tuna, salt and pepper. Spread mixture in a 13"x9" baking pan sprayed with non-stick vegetable spray. Cover with crushed chips. Bake, uncovered, at 350 degrees for 30 to 45 minutes, until hot and bubbly. Watch closely, so chips don't burn. Makes 8 servings.

Take it easy when planning holiday dinners...stick to tried & true recipes! Guests are often just as happy with simple comfort foods as with the most elegant gourmet meal.

Nonna's Christmas Eve Spaghetti *Sharon Velenosi*
Costa Mesa, CA

My Nonna made this traditional Christmas Eve dish every year. We couldn't wait to sit down to it! It is one of the special joys and memories of Nonna that we continue every Christmas Eve.

2 7-oz. cans tuna packed in olive oil, drained and oil reserved
2-oz. can flat fillets of anchovies, drained

2 cloves garlic, finely minced
Optional: 1 T. olive oil
28-oz. can tomato purée
32-oz. pkg. spaghetti, uncooked and divided

Combine tuna and anchovies in a bowl; finely mince together and set aside. In a skillet over medium heat, sauté garlic in reserved oil until soft. Add tuna mixture; sauté for about 2 minutes, adding the extra olive oil if necessary. Stir in tomato purée. Reduce heat to low. Cover and simmer for 30 minutes, adding a little water if a thinner sauce is desired. Meanwhile, cook 3/4 of spaghetti according to package directions, reserving the rest for another recipe; drain. Serve sauce over cooked spaghetti. Makes 6 to 8 servings.

Stick adhesive-backed gold stars onto plain pillar candles for a holiday centerpiece that's so quick, it's child's play.

Nona's Easy Manicotti

Eleanor Dionne
Beverly, MA

This is a favorite holiday recipe handed down by my mom 40 years ago. It's simple because you stuff the uncooked shells. Serve the manicotti with meatballs or sausage, as you like.

2 32-oz. jars spaghetti sauce, divided
32-oz. container ricotta cheese
16-oz. pkg. shredded mozzarella cheese

8-oz. container grated Parmesan or Romano cheese
5 to 6 eggs, beaten
24 manicotti pasta shells, uncooked

Pour one jar sauce into a greased 13"x9" baking pan. Spread sauce to cover bottom of pan; set aside. In a large bowl, combine cheeses and eggs; mix well. Stuff uncooked shells with cheese mixture, using a cake decorating tube or a knife. Arrange shells side-by-side in the pan as they're filled. Cover shells with remaining jar of sauce. Cover pan tightly with aluminum foil. Bake at 400 degrees for 50 to 60 minutes, until bubbly and shells are tender. Makes 8 to 10 servings.

Keep all of your family's favorite holiday story books in a basket by a cozy chair. Set aside one night as family night to read your favorites together.

Spicy Roasted Red Pepper Pasta

Marie Matter
Dallas, TX

This simple pasta dish is so flavorful, you won't believe how easy it is! If you'd prefer to tone down the spice, simply eliminate the cayenne and red pepper flakes.

16-oz. pkg. orechiette or rotini
  pasta, uncooked
12-oz. jar roasted red peppers,
  drained
1/2 c. milk
1/2 t. garlic powder
1/2 t. onion powder
1/4 t. kosher salt
1/4 t. pepper
1/4 t. red pepper flakes
1/8 t. cayenne pepper
1/4 c. shredded Pecorino
  Romano cheese
3 T. fresh Italian parsley,
  chopped

Cook pasta according to package directions; drain and return to cooking pot. Meanwhile, combine red peppers, milk and seasonings in a blender or food processor. Process until smooth. Adjust seasonings as desired. Pour red pepper sauce over cooked pasta; toss to coat. Serve in bowls, topped with cheese and parsley. Makes 4 servings.

Turn Christmas cards into festive napkin rings. Cut them into wide strips with decorative-edge scissors, join ends with craft glue and add a sprig of faux holly...simple!

Carly's Pot o' Beans

Carly St. Clair
Lynnwood, WA

This is comfort food at our home. On a cold autumn or winter evening after a long day at work, it's heavenly to come home to the aroma of these beans simmering in the slow cooker. Serve with homemade cornbread or biscuits.

2 16-oz. pkgs. dried pinto
  beans
1-1/2 c. celery with leaves,
  chopped
3 carrots, peeled and chopped,
  or 1 c. baby carrots, chopped

1 onion, chopped
8 c. chicken broth
1 env. ham seasoning
  concentrate
1 t. garlic powder
1/4 t. pepper

In a large bowl, cover dried beans with water. Let soak overnight. In the morning, drain and rinse beans. Add beans to a slow cooker sprayed with non-stick vegetable spray. Add celery, carrots and onion; pour broth over all. Add remaining ingredients; stir until blended. Cover and cook on high setting for 6 to 8 hours, until beans are soft. Makes 12 servings.

Gather everyone for a fireside meal...so cozy on a snowy day! Cook hot dogs on long forks or use pie irons to make pocket pies. You can even roast foil-wrapped potatoes in the coals. Make s'mores for a sweet ending.

Save Room
for Dessert

Southern Peanut Butter Pie

Carolyn Deckard
Bedford, IN

This recipe was found written in the back of my grandma's old cookbook. Our family has shared it many times over the years.

2/3 c. sugar
1 c. creamy peanut butter
1/2 t. salt

3 eggs, beaten
1 c. dark corn syrup
9-inch pie crust

In a bowl, combine all ingredients except pie crust; pour mixture into unbaked crust. Bake at 375 degrees for one hour. Center may be slightly soft but will become firm as the pie cools. Cool completely before cutting. Serves 6.

Grandma's Foolproof Pie Crust

Lisa Hartz
Washington, IN

Grandma always rolled out her own crusts from this recipe. She used to bake me a little "extra" flat crust, topped with cinnamon-sugar.
I still love her crust more than the pies themselves!

4 c. all-purpose flour
1 T. sugar
2 t. salt
1-3/4 c. shortening

1 egg. beaten
1/2 c. water
1 T. vinegar

In a large bowl, stir together flour, sugar and salt with a fork. Cut in shortening until crumbly. Beat egg in a small bowl. Stir in water and vinegar; add to flour mixture. Stir until moistened and a soft dough forms. Divide into 5 portions; wrap with plastic wrap. Refrigerate at least 30 minutes before using. Chilled dough may be taken from the refrigerator and rolled at once. May also freeze for later use; thaw until soft enough to roll out. Makes 5 single crusts.

For a crisp, golden top crust, brush with water and sprinkle with sugar before popping the pie into the oven.

Nanny's Fudge Pie

Delana Jean
Covington, TX

This recipe was given to me by my Nanny. It is so quick & easy to make, even on the spur of the moment for unexpected guests. They will want seconds and will ask you for the recipe.

1/2 c. butter, melted
1 c. sugar
1/2 c. all-purpose flour
2 T. baking cocoa
2 eggs, beaten

1/2 to 1 t. vanilla extract
Optional: 1/2 c. chopped pecans
Garnish: vanilla ice cream,
    chocolate syrup

In a large bowl, combine all ingredients except garnish; mix well. Pour mixture into a greased 9" pie plate. Bake at 350 degrees for 20 minutes. Serve slices topped with a scoop of ice cream and a drizzle of chocolate syrup. Makes 8 servings.

Make grown-ups feel like kids again! Stuff stockings with penny candy, comic books, card games and other childhood delights... hang from the backs of dining room chairs with tasseled cords.

Christmas Blackberry Pie

Kim Hinshaw
Cedar Park, TX

When our children were young, I wanted to enjoy the holidays with them and not feel rushed. So I did as much for Christmas dinner ahead of time as I could. This pie can be made ahead and frozen. It's yummy made with raspberries, strawberries or sliced peaches too.

3 c. fresh or frozen blackberries
1 c. sugar
3 T. cornstarch
1 T. lemon juice
8-oz. pkg. cream cheese,
    softened

3/4 c. powdered sugar
1 t. vanilla extract
8-oz. container whipping cream
9-inch graham cracker crust,
    baked

In a large bowl, cover berries with sugar; set aside for 30 minutes. Transfer berry mixture to a saucepan; add cornstarch. Cook over medium-low heat, stirring often, until syrup is thickened and clear. Remove from heat; stir in lemon juice. Set aside to cool. Meanwhile, beat cream cheese in a separate bowl until smooth. Add powdered sugar and vanilla; mix well and set aside. In another bowl, with an electric mixer on high speed, whip cream until soft peaks form. Gently fold whipped cream into cream cheese mixture; spoon mixture into baked crust. Spread blackberry glaze over filling. Cover and chill several hours to overnight. May be frozen; thaw in refrigerator. Serves 6 to 8.

A fresh-baked pie looks so pretty presented in an old-fashioned glass pie plate. Wrap it up in clear cellophane and use a favorite black & white photo for a gift tag.

Save Room *for* Dessert

Raspberry Buttermilk Pie

JoAnn Kurtz
Castaic, CA

I tried this pie at a restaurant here in town and figured I could make it at home. It tastes wonderful and is inexpensive to make... what more could you want?

1/2 c. butter, room temperature
1-1/2 c. sugar
1 T. all-purpose flour
3 eggs, beaten
1 c. buttermilk
1 t. vanilla extract

1/8 t. nutmeg
1 c. fresh raspberries
9-inch pie crust
Garnish: whipped cream,
    additional raspberries

Combine butter and sugar in a bowl. With a wooden spoon, beat until smooth. Add flour and eggs; stir until thoroughly combined. Stir in buttermilk, vanilla and nutmeg. Fold in berries; spoon mixture into unbaked pie crust. Bake at 350 degrees for 40 to 45 minutes. Cool completely before serving. Garnish with whipped cream and more berries. Makes 6 to 8 servings.

Spread out cotton batting as a snowy setting for tiny vintage houses and reindeer or snowman figures...what a sweet centerpiece! Add a dash of mica flakes for icy sparkle.

Wacky Cake

*Patricia Wick
Akron, NY*

*A simple chocolatey dessert Mother used to make. Mix it, bake it,
serve it all using one pan. Absolutely delicious...a family favorite
for generations!*

1-1/2 c. all-purpose flour
1 c. sugar
1/2 c. baking cocoa
1 t. baking soda
1/2 t. salt

6 T. oil
1 T. vinegar
1 t. vanilla extract
1 c. cold water

Sift flour, sugar, cocoa, baking soda and salt into an ungreased
11"x7" or 9"x9" baking pan. Make 3 wells in flour mixture: one large,
one medium and one small. Add oil to large well. Add vinegar to
medium well. Add vanilla to small well. Cover all with cold water;
mix all together thoroughly with a fork. Bake at 350 degrees for
25 minutes. Allow cake to cool completely in pan. Frost with
Buttercream Frosting; cut into squares. Makes 6 to 8 servings.

Buttercream Frosting:

1/4 c. butter, softened
few drops vanilla extract

2 c. powdered sugar
1 to 3. T. milk

Combine butter and vanilla in a bowl. Add powdered sugar; stir until
smooth. Add milk, a little at a time, to make a creamy consistency.

Add a sweet touch to holiday desserts with chocolate curls!
Use a vegetable peeler to slice thin strips of chocolate from a
chocolate bar and place them on top of frosted cakes
and cream pies.

Grandma Power's Oatmeal Cake
Terri Lock
Carrollton, MO

This recipe is like a warm pudding...great to enjoy on a cold winter day!
My grandmother shared so much love with her family and especially
when she baked her wonderful desserts.

1 c. long-cooking oats,
  uncooked
1-1/2 c. water
1/2 c. plus 2 T. butter, softened
  and divided
1 c. sugar
1-3/4 c. brown sugar, packed
  and divided

2 eggs
1-1/3 c. all-purpose flour
1 t. baking soda
1/2 t. salt
1/2 t. cinnamon
1/4 c. evaporated milk
1/4 c. sweetened flaked coconut

Cook oats with water as directed on package; set aside to cool. In a bowl, blend together 1/2 cup butter, sugar and 3/4 cup brown sugar; stir in eggs, one at a time. In a separate bowl, sift together flour, baking soda, salt and cinnamon. Add flour mixture to butter mixture alternately with oat mixture; stir well. Pour batter into a 9" deep-dish pie plate. Bake, uncovered, at 350 degrees for one hour. Meanwhile, in a separate bowl, mix together remaining butter, remaining brown sugar, evaporated milk and coconut. Spread on cake. Broil cake until topping is bubbly and golden. Cut into squares. Serves 6 to 8.

A hug is the perfect gift...one size fits all,
and nobody minds if you exchange it.
–Ivern Ball

Apple Spice Cake

Marie King
Independence, MO

One day I wanted some of my grandma's applesauce raisin spice cookies, but didn't want to make cookies. So I started adding ingredients and came up with this recipe. It was a huge hit! It is really good warm, right out of the oven...even better the next day!

18-1/4 oz. pkg. spice cake mix
15-oz. can unsweetened
   applesauce
2 eggs, beaten

1 Gala apple, peeled, cored
   and diced
1/2 c. raisins
1/4 c. pecans, chopped

In a large bowl, beat together dry cake mix, applesauce and eggs. Stir in apple, raisins and pecans. Mix until combined. Spread batter evenly in a greased 13"x9" glass baking pan. Bake at 350 degrees for 45 to 50 minutes. Cake will be moist and not quite done in the very center. Remove from oven; let cool for 5 minutes. Meanwhile, make Vanilla-Caramel Glaze; drizzle over warm cake. Let cool for 25 to 30 minutes before serving. Serves 20.

Vanilla-Caramel Glaze:

3/4 c. powdered sugar
1 T. caramel ice cream topping

1-1/2 t. vanilla extract
2 to 4 T. water

Combine powdered sugar, topping and vanilla; mix well. Stir in water, one tablespoon at a time, until glaze coats the back of spoon.

Mix up some mulling spice bags! Fill a small muslin bag with one teaspoon each of whole cloves, allspice and orange zest plus two or three cinnamon sticks. To use, simmer the spice bag in 2 quarts apple cider for a hot beverage that will warm you right up.

Save Room *for Dessert*

Butterscotch Spice Hand Cake
Faye Lengenfelder
Renton, WA

I've made this recipe many years for my three boys. This cake is easy to make and you can eat it out of hand...great for snacking!

3-1/2 oz. pkg. cook & serve
  butterscotch pudding mix
2 c. milk

15-1/4 oz. pkg. spice cake mix
6-oz. pkg. butterscotch chips
1 c. chopped nuts

In a large saucepan, combine dry pudding mix and milk; cook according to package directions. Add dry cake mix to hot pudding; stir until well mixed. Pour batter into a 13"x9" baking pan sprayed with non-stick vegetable spray. Sprinkle with butterscotch chips and nuts. Bake at 350 degrees for 30 minutes. Cool; cut into squares. Serves 12.

When I was little, as I got older I was allowed to stay up later on Christmas Eve. One year we had new neighbors. My grandparents were sitting up one night talking about how they noticed the neighbors didn't have a tree or gifts but were trying to have a good Christmas. I told my grandma that we should give them our Christmas, and after discussing it with my little sisters we decided to do it. Late that night Poppa took our little tree over with an extension cord and quietly set it up on their porch. We carried over all of our gifts except one each that we'd picked to keep for ourselves. Grandmother penned a note "from Santa" to say he'd noticed they had no chimney, so he'd left their things on the porch. The next day, my family had the best Christmas ever and so did our neighbors and their girls. That night they shared our dinner. Our families have been great friends ever since.

–April Lovelady, Diboll, TX

Cranberry-Pecan White Chocolate Pie

Pam Moore
Luna Pier, MI

I've made this scrumptious family favorite for Thanksgiving and Christmas the past ten years or more. Light brown sugar may be used, but I have found that dark brown sugar gives it a richer taste.

1 c. fresh cranberries
1 c. pecan halves
1 c. white chocolate chips
9-inch pie crust
3 eggs, beaten

3/4 c. dark brown sugar, packed
3/4 c. light corn syrup
2 T. all-purpose flour
1 t. orange zest

Layer cranberries, pecans and chocolate chips in unbaked pie crust; set aside. In a bowl, stir together remaining ingredients; blend well and pour into crust. Set pie plate on a baking sheet. Bake at 400 degrees for 25 minutes. Remove from oven; cover pie with a piece of aluminum foil coated with non-stick vegetable spray. Bake an additional 10 to 15 minutes, until crust is golden and filling is set in center. Makes 8 servings.

As Christmas nears, plan a family slumber party! Set up quilts and sleeping bags around the tree, pass around lots of snacks and watch a holiday movie. Before falling asleep, read "The Night Before Christmas" with only the tree lights on.

Save Room *for Dessert*

Mom's 75-Dollar Pecan Pie

Sylvia Ratley
Branson, MO

Lots of bakers have a great pecan pie recipe, but this one is firmer and not as gooey as most. My 93-year-old mom got this recipe over 50 years ago from a dear friend at church and added her special touches. This pie was recently auctioned at my sister's school for 75 dollars. Enjoy!

3/4 c. sugar
3/4 c. dark corn syrup
1-1/2 T. all-purpose flour
1-1/2 to 2 T. butter, melted and
   slightly cooled

3 eggs, beaten
1 t. vanilla extract
1 c. pecan halves
9-inch pie crust

Combine all ingredients except pecans and pie crust in a large bowl. Mix well; stir in pecans. Pour mixture into unbaked pie crust. Bake at 325 degrees for 40 to 50 minutes, until golden and a knife tip inserted in the center comes out clean. Cool before slicing. Makes 6 to 8 servings.

Christmas tree farms sometimes offer rides in
horse-drawn sleighs or wagons...take the family for
a ride they'll never forget!

Raisin Crumb Pie

Karen Hood Keeney
Bronston, KY

This pie is my mom's favorite. The crunchy topping makes it extra delicious. When I served it in my restaurant, Karen's Konfections and Deli, there was never a crumb left. Once they've tasted it, everyone wants the recipe!

1-1/2 c. raisins
9-inch deep-dish pie crust
1/2 c. evaporated milk
2 eggs, beaten

2 c. sugar, divided
1/3 c. plus 1/2 c. all-purpose
   flour, divided
1/3 c. cold butter

Place raisins into unbaked pie crust; set aside. In a small bowl, combine evaporated milk, eggs, 1-1/2 cups sugar and 1/3 cup flour. Stir until blended; pour over raisins and set aside. In a separate bowl, mix together remaining sugar, remaining flour and butter with a fork until crumbly. Sprinkle over mixture in pie crust. Bake at 350 degrees for 50 to 60 minutes. Cool before slicing. Makes 8 servings.

For plump, juicy raisins, cover them with boiling water and let stand for 15 minutes. Drain and pat dry with a paper towel before adding to the recipe.

Save Room for Dessert

Mom's Pumpkin Pie

Jan Abney
Salem, MO

My mom's pumpkin pie was always the favorite dessert on the table at every Thanksgiving and Christmas dinner. I miss my mom, but am so glad to have her recipes.

3 c. fresh pumpkin, cooked and
  sieved, or canned pumpkin
2 12-oz. cans evaporated milk
2 c. brown sugar, packed
4 eggs, beaten

2 T. pumpkin pie spice
4 t. cinnamon
1 t. salt
3 8-inch pie crusts

In a large bowl, combine all ingredients except pie crusts. Beat well with an electric mixer on medium speed or by hand. Pour into unbaked pie crusts. Bake at 425 degrees for 15 minutes. Reduce heat to 350 degrees; bake an additional 35 minutes. Makes 3 pies; each serves 6 to 8.

Keep a tin of pumpkin pie spice handy for baking. A blend of cinnamon, ginger, nutmeg and cloves, it's delicious in sweet breads and biscuits, not just pies!

Granny's Grated Sweet Potato Pudding

Shirl Parsons
Cape Carteret, NC

This delicious recipe has been in my husband's family for generations. It was handed down from his great-grandma to his grandma and shared with many in her self-published cookbook.

4 c. sweet potatoes, peeled
   and grated
2 c. sugar
12-oz. can evaporated milk
4 eggs, beaten

1/3 c. butter, melted and
   slightly cooled
1/2 t. allspice
1/2 t. cinnamon

Combine all ingredients in a large bowl; mix well. Pour into a lightly greased 3-quart casserole dish. Bake, uncovered, at 350 degrees for one hour, or until set and center tests clean with a toothpick. Makes 6 servings.

Gran's Apple Crisp

Karen Nicholson
Beaconsfield, Quebec

This recipe was my great-grandmother's and has been passed down through the generations. It's a little different from most, as it doesn't use any oats. I have yet to meet someone who doesn't love it!

6 McIntosh apples, peeled, cored
   and sliced
3/4 c. brown sugar, packed

1/2 c. all-purpose flour
1/4 c. butter, sliced

Arrange apples in a buttered 2-quart casserole dish; set aside. In a separate bowl, mix brown sugar, flour and butter until crumbly. Sprinkle mixture over apples. Bake, uncovered, at 350 degrees for 30 to 40 minutes, until bubbly and golden. Serves 8.

To have good health throughout the next year,
eat an apple on Christmas Eve.

–Old saying

Save Room for Dessert

Easy-as-Pie Peach Cobbler

Miranda Ching
Aiea, HI

One of my most-used recipes for church potlucks and get-togethers! I usually have the ingredients on hand and almost everyone seems to like it. Try it with a cup of frozen blueberries or raspberries spread over the peaches before adding the batter. Either way, it's wonderful.

2 15-oz. cans sliced peaches, drained
1 c. self-rising flour
3/4 c. sugar
1/2 c. butter, melted and slightly cooled

2/3 c. milk
cinnamon-sugar or cinnamon to taste
Optional: vanilla ice cream

Spread peach slices evenly in a greased 9"x9" glass baking pan; set aside. In a bowl, combine flour, sugar, melted butter and milk; mix well. Pour mixture carefully over peaches; do not stir. Generously sprinkle with cinnamon-sugar or cinnamon. Bake, uncovered, at 350 degrees for 50 to 60 minutes, until fruit is bubbly and top is golden. Serve warm, topped with a scoop of ice cream, if desired. Makes 9 servings.

A basket of pine cone fire starters is a special gift. Carefully melt old candle ends in a double boiler and use tongs to dip pine cones. Sprinkle with a little glitter, if you like, then set on wax paper to dry.

Deluxe Apple Crunch

Susan Wilson
Johnson City, TN

My husband loves apple desserts and this simple recipe is a favorite of his. It's wonderful topped with a dollop of whipped cream...try it with a slice of Cheddar cheese too!

2 21-oz. cans apple pie filling
1/2 c. sugar
nutmeg or cinnamon to taste
1/2 c. butter
1 c. brown sugar, packed
1/2 c. all-purpose flour

1/2 c. long-cooking oats, uncooked
1/2 c. raisins
1/2 c. chopped pecans
Garnish: whipped cream or ice cream

Spread pie filling in a greased 9"x9" baking pan. Sprinkle with sugar and spice; set aside. In a bowl, combine remaining ingredients except garnish. Stir with a fork until mixture resembles coarse meal. Spread mixture over apples. Bake, uncovered, at 325 degrees for one hour. Serve warm, garnished as desired. Serves 8.

Place newly arrived Christmas cards in a napkin holder,
then take a moment every evening to share
happy holiday greetings over dessert!

Save Room *for Dessert*

Joey's Peach Dump Cake

Tina Hengen
Clarkston, WA

*I taught my very special nephew Joey to make this yummy
dessert. He was so proud of himself and deemed it one of
the best desserts he's ever had!*

2 29-oz. cans sliced peaches,
  divided
18-1/2 oz. pkg. white cake mix
1/2 c. butter, sliced

1 c. brown sugar, packed
2 t. cinnamon
1 c. chopped nuts

Pour one can of peaches with juice into a lightly greased 13"x9" baking
pan. Drain the remaining can; add peaches to pan. Sprinkle dry cake
mix over the top; dot with butter. Combine brown sugar with
cinnamon in a bowl; sprinkle over cake mix. Sprinkle nuts over top.
Do not stir. Bake, uncovered, at 350 degrees for one hour, or until
bubbly and golden. Makes 8 to 10 servings.

Fill a big glass jar with vintage-style
candies...guests of all ages will love
scooping out their favorites!

Gram's Blackberry Jam Cake

Zoe Bennett
Columbia, SC

A real old-fashioned favorite and a must at family gatherings.

1 t. baking soda
3 T. buttermilk
3/4 c. butter, softened
1 c. sugar
3 eggs, beaten
1 c. seedless blackberry jam

2 c. all-purpose flour, divided
1 t. cinnamon
1/2 t. nutmeg
1/2 t. ground cloves
Garnish: caramel or
   fluffy white frosting

In a cup, dissolve baking soda in buttermilk; set aside. In a large bowl, stir together butter and sugar. Add eggs, jam and one cup flour; mix well. Add soda mixture, spices and remaining flour; beat well. Spread batter in a greased and floured 13"x9" baking pan. Bake at 350 degrees for 35 to 40 minutes, until a toothpick tests clean. Cool; spread with frosting. Serves 10 to 12.

Mommaw's Caramel Frosting

Tina Goodpasture
Meadowview, VA

My Mommaw made this frosting for me to eat by itself. It's wonderful on cakes too. Every time I make this, I think of Mommaw and how much I enjoyed this treat with her.

1/2 c. butter, softened
1 c. dark brown sugar, packed
1/3 c. whipping cream
1 T. vanilla extract

16-oz. pkg. powdered sugar
Optional: additional whipping
   cream

Melt butter in a saucepan over medium-low heat. Add brown sugar and cream. Cook for about 2 minutes, until brown sugar dissolves. Remove from heat; add vanilla. Transfer mixture to a large bowl. With an electric mixer on low speed, beat in powdered sugar until smooth. If frosting is too thick, add more cream, one tablespoon at a time, to desired consistency. Makes 8 servings.

Christmas Cake

Margie High
Pottstown, PA

My mom received this recipe from her own mother...I've never had another cake like it. After cooking the raisins and dates, I can hardly wait for them to cool! The smell of the cloves is wonderful too. It's a not-too-sweet dessert that's good for breakfast too.

2 c. water	3 c. all-purpose flour
1-1/2 c. raisins	1 t. baking soda
2 c. chopped dates	1 t. cinnamon
2 c. sugar	1/2 t. ground cloves
5 T. shortening	1 c. chopped walnuts

Bring water to a boil in a large saucepan over medium heat. Stir in raisins, dates, sugar and shortening. Reduce heat to medium-low; simmer for 20 minutes. Remove from heat and let cool. Meanwhile, sift flour, baking soda and spices into a large bowl. Stir flour mixture into cooled raisin mixture; stir in walnuts. Divide batter between 2 well greased 9"x5" loaf pans. Place pans on center rack of oven. Fill an 8"x8" baking pan with 2 cups water and set on bottom rack. Bake at 325 degrees for 1-1/2 hours. Cool; turn out loaves. Makes 2 loaves.

A loaf of homemade quick bread is always a welcome gift!
Make sure it stays fresh and tasty...let the bread cool completely
before wrapping well in plastic wrap or aluminum foil.

Shoo-Fly Cake

Denise Evans
Moosic, PA

My mom and gram used to make Shoo-Fly Pie when I was growing up.
This recipe has the same great flavor and is easy to toss together.

1 t. baking soda
2 T. hot water
4 c. all-purpose flour
2 c. sugar

1 t. salt
1 c. margarine, softened
1 c. molasses
2 c. cold water

In a cup, dissolve baking soda in hot water; set aside. In a large bowl, mix flour, sugar and salt. Add margarine; mix with a fork until crumbly. Reserve one cup of crumb mixture for topping. To remaining crumb mixture, add molasses, cold water and soda mixture. Stir well; pour batter into a greased 13"x9" baking pan or 3 greased 9" pie plates. Sprinkle reserved crumb mixture over top. Bake at 350 degrees for 45 minutes; do not overbake. Serves 18.

Every year on Christmas Eve, I left Santa a cookie, some milk and a carrot for Rudolph. In return, Santa would leave me a letter along with the gifts he'd brought. He always thanked me for the delicious treats for himself and Rudolph, and also said that he had kept track of me during the year. Santa always praised an accomplishment of mine. One year it was for practicing Christmas carols on the organ (he especially liked "Jolly Old St Nicholas"!), or that I was trying so hard in math, and so on. For years, I didn't catch on that Santa was really my older brother Jim. It's actually sweeter to me now than if the letters had really been from Santa.

—Mary Ventresco, Glendale, WI

Sherry Cake

Nancy Hanson
Murrietta, CA

I have been making this wonderful cake for almost 50 years and it never disappoints! I always make it to use in my special English trifle at Christmas, but it's also wonderful with a nice hot cup of tea! I have been asked for this recipe at least 40 times over the years...it really is that good and so easy to make.

18-1/2 oz. pkg. yellow cake mix
5.1-oz. pkg. instant vanilla
   pudding mix

3/4 c. cream sherry
3/4 c. oil
4 eggs, beaten

Combine dry cake and pudding mixes in a large bowl; add remaining ingredients. Beat with an electric mixer on medium speed until well blended. Batter will be thick. Pour batter into a well greased and floured Bundt® pan. Bake at 350 degrees for 45 to 50 minutes, until a toothpick inserted near the center tests clean. Cool cake in pan for about 10 minutes; turn out onto a wire rack and cool completely. Cake freezes very well if wrapped in heavy-duty aluminum foil. Makes 10 to 12 servings.

To neatly frost a cake, tuck strips of wax paper under the bottom edges of the cake. Discard the paper when the frosting is set.

Cranberry Cream Pie

Janis Parr
Campbellford, Ontario

This is truly a decadent dessert to serve with Christmas dinner. It's a long-standing favorite in our family.

1/2 c. sugar
1 T. cornstarch
2 c. fresh or frozen cranberries
15 t. water, divided
9-inch pie crust, baked
1 env. unflavored gelatin

2 c. dairy eggnog
1/8 t. nutmeg
Optional: 5 t. rum
1/2 c. whipping cream
Garnish: additional cranberries

In a small heavy saucepan, combine sugar, cornstarch, cranberries and 5 teaspoons water. Cook over medium heat for 5 minutes, or until berries begin to pop. Remove from heat. Cool; pour into baked pie crust and set aside. In a small saucepan, sprinkle dry gelatin over remaining water. Let stand for 5 minutes to soften. Place saucepan over a bowl of hot water; stir until gelatin dissolves. Add gelatin mixture to a large bowl; stir in eggnog, nutmeg and rum, if using. Cover and chill until slightly thickened. In a separate bowl, with an electric mixer on high speed, whip cream until soft peaks form. Fold whipped cream into eggnog mixture; cover and chill until well set. Spoon eggnog mixture over cranberries. Cover and chill at least 2 hours. Garnish pie with additional berries. Do not freeze pie. Makes 8 servings.

Set a teeny-tiny snowman at each person's place...so cute!
Simply glue white pompoms together with craft glue,
then add faces and scarves clipped from bits of felt.

Aunt Bernice's French Coconut Pie

Connie Saunders
Hillsboro, KY

My aunt made this pie for our annual family reunions for many years. She graciously shared the recipe with me long ago, when I was still a young, inexperienced cook. Now I am the one who takes it to those same reunions. This pie has also become a favorite of mine to take to church potlucks and to donate to our local volunteer fire department for their annual fundraiser fish fry.

3 eggs, beaten
1-1/2 c. sugar
1/2 c. butter, melted and
   slightly cooled

1 T. vanilla extract
1 T. white vinegar
1 c. sweetened flaked coconut
9-inch deep-dish pie crust

In a large bowl, whisk together eggs, sugar and melted butter. Stir in vanilla, vinegar and coconut. Pour mixture into unbaked pie crust. To prevent overbrowning, place a strip of aluminum foil around rim of pie crust. Bake at 350 degrees for 45 to 60 minutes, removing foil after 15 minutes, until a knife tip inserted in the center tests clean. Cool before slicing. Makes 8 servings.

Decorate a small galvanized mailbox with ribbons, buttons and painted-on snowflakes. Add your name to each side with a paint pen in big bold letters...a whimsical holder for those holiday cards, photos and letters.

Grandma Beach's Fluffy Lemon Cheesecake

Pat Beach
Fisherville, KY

My husband's mother used to make this cheesecake at least once a week when he was growing up. The recipe has now been handed down to my husband's children. It's super easy to prepare and you'll love its light lemony flavor, so different from any other cheesecake you've ever had. Try it topped with cherry pie filling too.

2 c. graham cracker crumbs
1/2 c. margarine, melted
3-oz. pkg. lemon gelatin mix
1 c. boiling water
8-oz. pkg. cream cheese,
  softened

1 c. sugar
1 t. vanilla extract
5-oz. can evaporated milk,
  chilled
8-oz. can crushed pineapple,
  drained

In a bowl, combine cracker crumbs and melted margarine. Mix well; press into the bottom of an ungreased 13"x9" baking pan. In a separate large bowl, dissolve dry gelatin mix in boiling water. Stir well and let cool. In another bowl, blend cream cheese, sugar and vanilla. Stir cream cheese mixture into cooled gelatin. With an electric mixer on high speed, whip evaporated milk until stiff peaks form. Fold into cream cheese mixture; spoon over crust. Spread pineapple over top. Cover and refrigerate for 4 to 5 hours; cut into squares. Makes 12 to 16 servings.

Take-out boxes are available in lots of festive colors and patterns.
Keep some handy for wrapping up food gifts in a jiffy...and for
sending home dessert with guests who just can't eat another bite!

172

Save Room for Dessert

Cherry-Topped Cheesecake Pie

Vicki Meredith
Grandview, IN

Mom used to make this pie when I was growing up and it is so easy to make, it's fun to have the kids help. I have used it so often, the recipe in my book is getting yellowed and messy. I use a ready-made graham cracker crust when time is short. Yummy!

1 c. graham cracker crumbs
1/2 c. plus 3 T. sugar, divided
1/4 c. butter, softened
8-oz. pkg. cream cheese,
    softened

2 c. frozen whipped topping,
    thawed
3/4 c. canned cherry pie filling

In a bowl, combine cracker crumbs, 3 tablespoons sugar and butter; mix well. Press into the bottom and sides of an 8" pie plate. Cover and chill for one hour. In a separate bowl, beat cream cheese with remaining sugar until creamy. Fold in whipped topping; spoon into crust. Spread pie filling around the edges of pie. Cover and chill at least 3 hours. Serves 6 to 8.

Bundle up the kids and take a ride to see the holiday lights
around town. Bring cozy blankets, plump pillows...
the kids can even wear their jammies!

Banana Pudding Trifle

Lisa Langston
Conroe, TX

This delicious dessert is similar to old-fashioned banana pudding, made with pound cake instead of vanilla wafers.

8-oz. pkg. cream cheese,
  softened
14-oz. can sweetened
  condensed milk
2-1/2 c. milk
5-oz. pkg. instant vanilla
  pudding mix

2 t. vanilla extract
16-oz. container frozen whipped
  topping, thawed and divided
12-oz. loaf pound cake, cubed
  and divided
5 to 6 ripe bananas, sliced
  and divided

In a large bowl, beat cream cheese with an electric mixer on medium speed until fluffy. Add milks, dry pudding mix and vanilla; beat until smooth and combined. With a spoon, gently fold in 1-1/2 cups whipped topping. Spoon half of pudding mixture into a glass serving bowl; layer with half each of cake cubes and banana slices. Repeat layering; add remaining whipped topping. Cover and chill for 4 hours to overnight, until set. Makes 10 servings.

Evaporated milk and sweetened condensed milk were both old standbys in Grandma's day. They're still handy today, but while they're both shelf-stable whole milk, they're not interchangeable. Condensed milk contains sugar and is cooked down to a thickened consistency, while evaporated milk is thinner and contains no added sugar.

Save Room *for Dessert*

Just Delightful Dessert

Wendy Ball
Battle Creek, MI

*My mother and grandmothers taught me many, many cooking tips.
My favorite is to make a dessert that can be popped in the oven just as
we're all sitting down for dinner. This scrumptious treat is that kind of
easy dessert.*

2 21-oz. cans apple, cherry,
  peach or blueberry pie filling
1 c. sweetened flaked coconut
1 c. chopped pecans

9-oz. pkg. white cake mix
1/2 c. butter, melted
Garnish: vanilla ice cream

Lightly spray a 15"x10" jelly-roll pan with non-stick vegetable spray.
Spread pie filling in pan; set aside. In a bowl, combine coconut, pecans
and dry cake mix; stir well. Sprinkle coconut mixture evenly over pie
filling; drizzle with melted butter. Bake, uncovered, at 350 degrees for
25 to 30 minutes, until bubbly and golden on top. Serve warm with a
scoop of ice cream. Makes 12 to 14 servings.

Grandma always said, "Never return a dish empty." Christmas is
a perfect time to gather up casserole dishes and pie plates that
have been left behind, fill with homebaked goodies
and return to their owners!

Grandpa's Bread Pudding

Megan Roehrer
Ortonville, MI

*Every Christmas my grandpa would make this simple treat for
all his grandchildren. I couldn't imagine a year going by
without his bread pudding on the dessert table!*

4 eggs, beaten
1 c. sugar
1 t. vanilla extract
5 c. milk

1/2 loaf seedless French bread,
cut into 1-inch cubes
nutmeg to taste

In a large bowl, whisk together eggs, sugar and vanilla. Add milk;
whisk again. Add bread cubes; stir until moistened and spoon into a
lightly greased 13"x9" baking pan. Sprinkle with nutmeg. Bake,
uncovered, at 350 degrees for 45 minutes. Serves 8 to 10.

Clear Sauce

Joyce Borrill
Utica, NY

*A delicious warm sauce to serve drizzled over
bread pudding and apple crisp.*

2 T. butter, sliced
2 T. all-purpose flour
1 c. water

3/4 c. sugar
1 t. vanilla extract

Melt butter in a small saucepan over low heat. Stir in flour until
smooth. Gradually add water, sugar and vanilla; bring to a boil. Cook
and stir for 2 minutes, or until sauce thickens. Serve warm. Makes
one cup.

A touch of whimsy...use Grandma's old cow-shaped
cream pitcher to top desserts with sauce.

Save Room *for* Dessert

Willie Mae's Apple Cobbler

Lynnette Jones
East Flat Rock, NC

My mother-in-law shared this recipe with me many, many years ago. It is quick and delicious. No one will ever guess the top crust is made of white bread!

6 to 7 slices white bread,
   crusts trimmed
6 c. Golden Delicious or Rome
   apples, peeled, cored
   and sliced
1 T. cinnamon

1 egg, beaten
1 c. sugar
1 T. all-purpose flour
1/2 c. butter, melted and
   slightly cooled

Cut each slice of bread into 3 equal pieces; set aside. Arrange sliced apples in a greased 13"x9" baking pan; sprinkle with cinnamon. Arrange bread pieces over apples. In a bowl, stir together egg, sugar, flour and melted butter; spoon over top. Bake, uncovered, at 350 degrees for 35 minutes, or until golden on top. Serves 8 to 10.

How my Grandma Helen loved Christmas! She has been gone now for 50 years, but I still remember the bayberry scent wafting from the tapers in her candelabra and the sweet taste of the sparkly gumdrops in the glass bowl on her old oak buffet. Most of all I remember the pretty tree she decorated with glass balls, strands of silver tinsel and bubble lights in hues of many colors. As a rule, Grandma never lit her tree in the daytime except on Christmas. One late afternoon in December Grandma plugged in her tree and adjusted the bubble lights so all were upright. She took my hand and led me over to the stiff old leather couch where we sat side-by-side waiting for the lights to start bubbling. I remember the warm glow that filled the room and enfolded us that long-ago December as I sat drinking in the beauty of Grandma's Christmas tree and basking in the warmth of her love.

–Helen Thoen, Manly, IA

Sludge Pudding

Bethanna Kortie
Greer, SC

My mom used to make Fudge Batter Pudding when I was growing up and it was one of my favorites. A few years ago I asked her for the recipe so that my family could enjoy it, too. One day, my daughter made it for company. I was horrified when I saw the results...it was pitch-black! Then I realized she'd used dark chocolate cocoa, not regular baking cocoa. Our guests said the pudding looked like motor oil, but tasted delicious! We have now dubbed it "Sludge Pudding."

2 T. butter, melted
1 c. sugar, divided
1 t. vanilla extract
1 c. all-purpose flour
1 t. baking powder
3/4 t. salt, divided

8 T. dark chocolate baking
  cocoa, divided
1/2 c. milk
1-2/3 c. boiling water
Garnish: vanilla ice cream

In a large bowl, blend together butter, 1/2 cup sugar and vanilla; set aside. In a separate bowl, sift together flour, baking powder, 1/2 teaspoon salt and 3 tablespoons cocoa. Add flour mixture to butter mixture alternately with milk; stir well and set aside. In another bowl, combine boiling water and remaining sugar, cocoa and salt; spoon mixture into a greased 10"x6" baking pan. Drop batter over hot cocoa mixture by tablespoonfuls. Bake, uncovered, at 350 degrees for 40 to 45 minutes. Serve warm, topped with a scoop of ice cream. Makes 6 servings.

Campfires, toasted marshmallows and ghost stories are
a classic combination. Why not whip up a batch of s'mores
to snack on and gather the family by the fireplace for
a reading of *A Christmas Carol*?

Eggnog Trifle

Mary Plut
Hackettstown, NJ

I always forget to serve eggnog at the holidays when I am so busy
with preparing the meal. This is a way to enjoy eggnog as
a dessert and pleases the non-chocolate fans!

1-1/2 c. whipping cream
3/4 c. cold milk
3.4-oz. pkg. instant vanilla
   pudding mix
2 c. dairy eggnog
1/2 t. almond extract
10-1/2 oz. loaf angel food
   cake or sponge cake, sliced
   1/2-inch thick and divided

1 c. seedless raspberry jam,
   divided
2 T. powdered sugar
1/2 t. vanilla extract
Garnish: maraschino cherry
   halves, nutmeg

In a deep bowl, with an electric mixer on high speed, whip cream
until soft peaks form; set aside. In a separate bowl, whisk together
milk and dry pudding mix until blended. Gradually add eggnog; mix
well. Fold in almond extract and one cup whipped cream; set aside.
Arrange 1/4 of cake slices in a 2-quart glass serving bowl; top with
1/3 cup jam. Spoon one cup eggnog mixture over all. Repeat layers
twice. Fold powdered sugar and vanilla into remaining whipped
cream; spoon over top. Cover and chill for at least 2 hours. Garnish
with cherries and a sprinkle of nutmeg. Makes 8 to 10 servings.

Are the kids getting cabin fever on a snowy day? Send 'em
outdoors with bottles of colored water to squirt
holiday messages on the freshly fallen snow.

Vintage Christmas Poke Cake

Tina Butler
Royse City, TX

My favorite recipes have always been vintage ones, because they remind me so much of my childhood. Refrigerator cakes date back as far as our grandmothers and are still a favorite in many households, including mine. The green and red colors are perfect for Christmas.

18-1/2 oz. pkg. French vanilla
  or white cake mix
2 c. boiling water, divided
3-oz. pkg. strawberry gelatin
  mix

3-oz. pkg. lime gelatin mix
16-oz. container frozen whipped
  topping, thawed
Garnish: holiday sprinkles

Prepare cake mix according to package directions; bake batter in 2 greased 8" or 9" round cake pans. Cool; turn cakes out of pans and remove, right-side up, to clean 8" or 9" cake pans. Pierce cakes with a large fork at 1/2-inch intervals; set aside. In a bowl, mix one cup boiling water and dry strawberry gelatin mix. Stir 2 minutes, until completely dissolved. Slowly pour 3/4 of strawberry gelatin over one cake; discard remaining gelatin. Repeat with remaining boiling water, lime gelatin mix and second cake. Cover; refrigerate cakes for 3 to 4 hours. Shortly before serving time, remove cakes from refrigerator. Carefully dip bottoms of cake pans into warm water for 10 seconds to release cakes from pans. Assemble and frost layer cake with whipped topping; decorate with sprinkles. Chill cake at least one hour before serving. Makes 16 servings.

For a special Christmas dessert, bake your favorite layer cake, decorate it with birthday candles and sing happy birthday to Jesus!

Save Room for Dessert

Grandma's Creamy Cherry Dessert
Teri Lindquist
Gurnee, IL

Every Christmas we could count on finding this delicious dessert on our holiday table, and there was never a crumb left! It has been in our family since the 1960s...no dessert comes close to it. Serve with a cup of hot coffee or tea for a perfect ending to a holiday meal.

1-3/4 c. graham cracker crumbs, divided
1/4 c. light brown sugar, packed
1 T. all-purpose flour
1/4 c. butter, melted
2 8-oz. pkgs. cream cheese, softened
3 eggs, beaten
3/4 c. sugar
1 t. vanilla extract
1 to 2 21-oz. cans cherry pie filling
12-oz. container frozen whipped topping, thawed

In a bowl, blend together 1-1/2 cups cracker crumbs, brown sugar, flour and melted butter. Pat into the bottom of a 13"x9" baking pan coated with non-stick vegetable spray; set aside. In a separate large bowl, beat together cream cheese, eggs, sugar and vanilla. Spoon mixture over crust. Bake, uncovered, at 350 degrees for 20 minutes. Let cool. Spoon pie filling over cooled layer; spread with whipped topping. Sprinkle with remaining cracker crumbs. Serves 9 to 12.

Perhaps this year, one of Santa's elves will make an appearance in your home! Set out a small elf doll early in December to "monitor" good behavior. At night, the elf reports back to the North Pole, and the next morning can usually be found sitting in a different spot.

Bee Hive Dessert

Kathy Courington
Canton, GA

*Every Christmas my sister and I would request this dessert. It was
always a family favorite and so festive...nice and light too after
a heavy holiday meal. I hope you enjoy it too!*

3.4-oz. pkg. instant lemon
  pudding mix
2 c. milk
2 angel food cakes, sliced
  and divided

16-oz. container frozen whipped
  topping, thawed
16-oz. jar maraschino cherries,
  well drained and halved

In a large bowl, whisk dry pudding mix and milk for 2 minutes, until
thickened. Set aside for 5 minutes. Meanwhile, line a deep bowl with
wax paper all the way to top. Use 1/3 of cake slices to line bowl to
top. Spoon in half of pudding; top with another 1/3 of cake slices.
Repeat layers, ending with cake. Cover and refrigerate 8 hours to
overnight. To serve, invert bowl onto a serving platter; peel off wax
paper. Cover with whipped topping; decorate all over with cherries.
Return to refrigerator if not serving immediately. May also be layered
in a 13"x9" glass baking pan. Serves 12.

A speedy gift for a crafty friend! Fill a Mason jar with
vintage buttons, mini thread spools and other sewing notions.
Top the lid with batting and a circle of homespun, add a few
pearl-headed pins and it's ready to give. She'll love it!

Grandma's
Christmas Cookies

Candy Cane Oatmeal Cookies

Laurie Anderson
Mount Prospect, IL

Our family has a wonderful tradition of baking Christmas cookies together every December. Five generations have participated in this family gathering. We start baking at 9 a.m. and continue into the evening. The best part is sampling all of the cookie dough! My grandma, whose birthday was on Christmas, started this tradition and we continue it in her honor. My mom first brought this tasty recipe to our special day 35 years ago.

1 c. butter, softened
2 t. vanilla extract
1/2 c. powdered sugar
2 T. water
2-1/2 c. all-purpose flour

1/2 t. salt
1-1/2 c. long-cooking oats,
    uncooked
Garnish: white and red
    decorator frosting

In a large bowl, beat butter and vanilla until creamy. Gradually add powdered sugar; beat until fluffy. Stir in water; set aside. In a separate bowl, mix together flour and salt. Add flour mixture to butter mixture; blend thoroughly. Stir in oats until blended and a stiff dough forms. Add more water by tablespoonfuls if dough is too stiff. Form dough into candy canes, using about 2 tablespoons dough per cookie. Place cookies on ungreased baking sheets. Bake at 325 degrees for 20 to 25 minutes. Remove cookies to wire racks; cool. Spread cooled cookies with white frosting; add stripes with red frosting. Makes 3 dozen.

Take the kids to a paint-your-own pottery shop.
They'll love decorating a plate and mug especially
for Santa's milk and cookies!

Granny's Soft Chocolate Drop Cookies

Karen Crooks
West Des Moines, IA

This is my granny's recipe from many years ago. Made with brown sugar and buttermilk, these cookies are soft with a distinctive chocolate flavor. Frost with your favorite chocolate or vanilla frosting...caramel and cherry frosting are fantastic also!

1/2 c. shortening
1 c. brown sugar, packed
1 egg, beaten
1 t. vanilla extract
1-1/2 c. all-purpose flour
1/2 t. baking soda

1/4 t. salt
1/2 c. buttermilk
2 1-oz. sqs. unsweetened
  baking chocolate
Garnish: chocolate or vanilla
  frosting

In a large bowl, blend shortening and brown sugar. Add egg and vanilla; beat well and set aside. In a separate bowl, combine flour, baking soda and salt. Add flour mixture to shortening mixture alternately with buttermilk; set aside. Place chocolate squares in a microwave-safe bowl. Microwave on high for one minute; stir until smooth. Add melted chocolate to dough; stir well. Drop dough by rounded teaspoonfuls onto lightly greased baking sheets. Bake at 350 degrees for 10 to 12 minutes. Cool on wire racks; frost. Makes 2 dozen.

Delightful vintage holiday cookie tins can often be found at tag sales...just pop in a parchment paper lining and they're ready to fill with goodies for gift giving.

Grandma June's 100 Best Cookies

Meri Hebert
Cheboygan, MI

This recipe from my mom is still a family favorite. It's a great way to use up small amounts of leftover baking ingredients.

1 c. sugar
1 c. brown sugar, packed
1 c. oil
1 c. margarine, softened
1 egg, beaten
1 t. vanilla extract
1 c. quick-cooking oats, uncooked

3-1/2 c. all-purpose flour
1 t. baking soda
1 t. cream of tartar
1 t. salt
1 c. crispy rice cereal
1 c. sweetened flaked coconut
1/2 c. chopped pecans

In a very large bowl, stir together sugars, oil, margarine, egg and vanilla; set aside. In a separate large bowl, mix oats, flour, baking soda, cream of tartar and salt. Add flour mixture to sugar mixture; stir well. Add remaining ingredients; mix well. Form dough into walnut-size balls. Place cookies on parchment paper-lined baking sheets. Flatten each with the bottom of a buttered and sugared glass. Bake at 350 degrees for 8 to 9 minutes, until lightly golden. Let cool on baking sheets for 5 minutes; remove to wire racks. Makes 100 cookies, about 8 dozen.

Check your cupboard for glass tumblers with pretty patterns on the bottom. Just dip the glass in butter and sugar, then press to flatten walnut-size balls of dough.

Grandma's
Christmas Cookies

Grandma's Chocolate Chip Bars
Peggy Buckshaw
Stow, OH

My grandma made these bar cookies every year for our family reunion. They were a special treat that we all looked forward to. I made these often for my children's after-school treats and now make them just for comfort, as they're so quick & easy.

18-1/2 oz. pkg. yellow or
   chocolate cake mix
2 eggs, beaten
1/2 c. oil
2 T. water

6-oz. pkg. semi-sweet or milk
   chocolate chips
1 c. chopped walnuts
Garnish: powdered sugar

Prepare dry cake mix with eggs, oil and water according to package directions. Add chocolate chips and walnuts to batter; mix well. Spread batter in an ungreased 13"x9" baking pan. Bake at 350 degrees for 25 to 30 minutes. Cool; cut into squares. Sprinkle with powered sugar. Makes 2 dozen.

Sugar Doodle Drops
Kellyjean Gettelfinger
Sellersburg, IN

These are our holiday go-to cookies. We take them to just about every gathering at Christmas time. They're so easy to make, the kids usually whip them up for all of their school events too.

18-1/2 oz. yellow or white cake
   mix
1-1/2 c. frozen whipped
   topping, thawed

1 egg, beaten
1 T. cinnamon
3 T. sugar

In a bowl, combine dry cake mix, whipped topping and egg. Mix well until moistened. In a separate small bowl, combine cinnamon and sugar. Form dough into one-inch balls; roll in cinnamon-sugar. Place cookies on ungreased baking sheets. Bake at 350 degrees for 10 minutes; cool. Makes 2 dozen.

Apricot Bars

Wendy Ball
Battle Creek, MI

My grandparents lived in California and grew an endless bounty of produce. Instead of sending fresh apricots through the mail, Grandma would send us jars of her mouthwatering homemade apricot preserves! Now I make these for the library bake sales and they sell quickly.

1-1/2 c. all-purpose flour
1 t. baking powder
1/4 t. salt
1 c. brown sugar, packed

1-1/2 c. quick-cooking oats, uncooked
1 c. butter
3/4 c. apricot preserves

In a large bowl, mix together flour, baking powder and salt; stir in brown sugar and oats. Cut in butter with a fork until crumbly. Pat 2/3 of crumb mixture into a 9"x9" inch baking pan coated with non-stick vegetable spray. Spread with preserves; cover with remaining crumb mixture. Bake at 375 degrees for 35 minutes, or until lightly golden. Cool. Cut into bars or squares. Makes 2-1/2 dozen.

For pretty stained-glass sugar cookies, use a mini cookie cutter to cut out a window in each cookie. Fill with crushed hard candy and bake at 300 degrees for 10 minutes, or until candy is melted.

Grandma's
Christmas Cookies

Grandma Gwen's Kolachis

Jennifer Ticknor
Cohoes, NY

When I was a child, Christmas dinner at my Grandma Gwen's house sometimes featured 25 to 30 dishes. So it was a challenge to save room for these flaky treats...somehow we always managed! As an adult, baking the Kolachis always transports me back to Grandma's bustling, overstuffed kitchen at holiday time. Truly the best place in the whole world.

8-oz. pkg. cream cheese, softened	1/2 c. brown sugar, packed
1-1/3 c. butter, softened	1/4 c. sugar
2-2/3 c. all-purpose flour	1 t. vanilla extract
2 c. chopped walnuts	1/2 c. milk
	Garnish: powdered sugar

In a bowl, beat cream cheese and butter until smooth. Add flour slowly until well blended. Form dough into 2 balls; cover and refrigerate for 2 hours to overnight. For nut filling, combine walnuts, sugars and vanilla in a food processor; process until finely ground. Add milk; pulse until well moistened. Cover and refrigerate until ready to use. Remove one dough ball from the refrigerator. On a surface sprinkled generously with powdered sugar, roll out until dough is very thin, about 1/8-inch thick. Cut dough into 4-inch by one-inch rectangles. Spoon 1/2 teaspoon nut filling across one narrow end; roll up, starting from nut end. Place cookies on ungreased baking sheets. Bake at 350 degrees for 12 minutes, or until lightly golden. Cool for 2 minutes on baking sheet; transfer cookies to a wire rack. Sprinkle with powered sugar. Repeat steps with second dough ball. Makes 4 dozen.

Invite friends over for an old-fashioned cookie exchange! It's a nice break from all the holiday hustle & bustle. Keep this get-together simple and have friends bring just a dozen cookies...enough for everyone to sample.

Chocolate Gingerbread Men

Gail Ebey
Canal Fulton, OH

My maternal grandmother grew up in Mississippi, bringing some of her southern recipes to Ohio to share with her family. These gingerbread cookies are a holiday staple that she shared with me. Now that she has passed on, I'd like to continue this old family tradition.

2 1-oz. sqs. unsweetened
   baking chocolate, chopped
1/2 c. shortening
1/2 c. molasses
2-1/2 c. all-purpose flour

2/3 c. sugar
1 t. baking soda
1/4 t. salt
1 t. ground ginger
1/4 c. milk

In the top of a double boiler, combine chocolate, shortening and molasses. Heat over hot water, stirring occasionally, until chocolate is melted and well combined. In a large bowl, combine remaining ingredients except milk. Add chocolate mixture; stir well and let cool. Add milk, stirring well. Pat dough into a ball; cover and refrigerate for about one hour. On a floured surface, roll out dough 1/4-inch thick. Cut out cookies with a greased gingerbread man cutter. Place cookies on parchment paper-lined baking sheets. Bake at 375 degrees for 6 minutes; cool on a wire rack. Makes 2 to 3 dozen.

Bake up a batch of gingerbread boys and girls, then let the kids decorate them! Set out a variety of small candies and tubs of frosting. You'll be amazed by how creative kids can be.

Grandma's
Christmas Cookies

Grandma's Old-Fashioned Brownies

Pearl Teiserskas
Brookfield, IL

When I was very young, we used to visit my grandmother in Florida for the holidays. It was wonderful to be able to travel to a warmer climate...and I always knew Grandmother's delicious chocolate brownies would be waiting for us when we arrived.

1/2 c. butter, melted	3/4 c. all-purpose flour
1/4 c. baking cocoa	1/8 t. salt
2 eggs	Optional: 1/2 c. chopped
1 c. sugar	walnuts

Combine melted butter and cocoa in a bowl; stir well and set aside. In a separate large bowl, beat eggs until frothy. Add remaining ingredients; mix well. Pour cocoa mixture over egg mixture; stir together. Pour batter into a greased 8"x8" baking pan. Bake at 350 degrees for 30 minutes. Cool; spread with Cocoa Icing and sprinkle with nuts, if desired. Cut into squares. Makes 8 to 10.

Cocoa Icing:

1-1/3 c. powdered sugar	3 T. butter
1/3 c. baking cocoa	2 T. hot water, divided

Combine powdered sugar, cocoa, butter and 1-1/3 tablespoons hot water. Beat until smooth, adding remaining water if needed.

Crushed candy canes make a festive topping for frosted brownies. Simply place in a plastic zipping bag and tap gently with a kitchen mallet until candy is broken up.

Dad's Radio Cookies

Peggy Donnally
Toledo, OH

My dad liked to cook and bake. Although he had mastered many of my grandmother's recipes, this one really stands out...he heard it on the radio. Only three ingredients and no flour! He was sure he'd heard wrong, so he mixed up a batch and...amazing cookies! He was so excited he called me right away. I still use this recipe when my nieces come to help me bake Christmas cookies. It's their favorite.

2 c. creamy peanut butter   2 eggs, beaten
2 c. sugar

Combine all ingredients in a bowl; mix well. Roll into one-inch balls and place on ungreased baking sheets. Lightly criss-cross each ball with the tines of a fork. Bake at 350 degrees for 8 minutes. Cool slightly before removing from baking sheets. Makes 4 dozen.

Great-Aunt Sandy's Chocolate No-Bake Cookies

Logan Perry
Trenton, FL

I'm sending you one of my favorite family recipes that I hope you will enjoy.

1/2 c. butter, sliced   1 t. vanilla extract
1/2 c. milk   1 c. creamy peanut butter
2 c. sugar   3 c. long-cooking oats,
3 T. plus 1 t. baking cocoa   uncooked

Combine butter, milk, sugar and cocoa in a large saucepan. Bring to a rolling boil over medium heat; boil for exactly 3 minutes. Remove from heat. Stir in vanilla and peanut butter; mix in oats. Spoon out by teaspoonfuls onto wax paper-lined baking sheets. Let stand for 30 minutes, or until set. Makes 1-1/4 to 2 dozen.

Want to keep cookies fresh longer? Simply place some crumpled tissue paper in the bottom of the cookie jar.

Granny's Ting-a-Lings

Stephanie Wren
La Vergne, TN

When I was a child, we would travel to see my mom's family in Oklahoma for Christmas. I remember Granny's house always being so warm and cozy and just a wonderful place to be. Her Ting-a-Lings were the one treat we always looked forward to, so she made sure she had a big ol' bowl ready for us. My brothers and I would gobble them up in no time.

12-oz. pkg. butterscotch chips
12-oz. can chow mein noodles
1 c. chopped peanuts

Optional: 1 c. mini
   marshmallows

Line baking sheets with wax paper; spray with non-stick vegetable spray and set aside. Melt butterscotch chips in the top of a double boiler over hot water. Stir in noodles, peanuts and marshmallows, if using. Drop mixture by teaspoonfuls onto wax paper-lined baking sheets. Let cool. Makes about 2 dozen.

Set aside a few cookies from each batch you bake. In no time at all, you can make up several platters of assorted cookies to drop off at a neighborhood firehouse, family shelter or retirement home. They're sure to be much appreciated.

Mom's Soft Raisin Cookies

Joyce Maltby
Cheboygan, MI

This was my mom's favorite cookie recipe. It makes a lot! When my sister and I were young, Mom said, "If you mix up the cookies, I will bake them for you." We just couldn't be bothered waiting around to bake them. Mom passed away ten days before Christmas 2013 at the age of 89. This recipe is a wonderful reminder of her.

2 c. raisins	1 t. baking powder
1 c. water	1 t. baking soda
1 c. shortening	1 t. salt
1-3/4 c. sugar	1/2 t. cinnamon
2 eggs, lightly beaten	1/2 t. nutmeg
1 t. vanilla extract	1/2 c. chopped walnuts
3-1/2 c. all-purpose flour	

In a saucepan over medium heat, combine raisins and water. Bring to a boil; cook and stir for 3 minutes. Remove from heat; cool but do not drain. In a large bowl, stir shortening until creamy; gradually stir in sugar. Stir in eggs and vanilla; set aside. In a separate bowl, combine flour, baking powder, baking soda, salt and spices. Add flour mixture to shortening mixture; mix well. Stir in walnuts and raisin mixture. Drop by teaspoonfuls onto greased baking sheets. Bake at 350 degrees for 12 to 14 minutes. Cool on wire racks. Makes 6 dozen.

A vintage tin lunchbox is just the right size to use as a cookie decorating kit. Cookie cutters, colored sugars and sprinkles will fit inside nicely...everything will be right at your fingertips when it's cookie-baking time!

Coconut-Cranberry Bars

Angela Davis
Guilford, IN

These bars are an awesome Christmasy treat and so easy to make. They're a crowd-pleaser wherever you may take them.

1-1/2 c. graham cracker crumbs
1/2 c. butter, melted
1-1/2 c. white chocolate chips
1-1/2 c. sweetened dried
   cranberries

14-oz. can sweetened
   condensed milk
1 c. sweetened flaked coconut
1 c. pecan halves

In a small bowl, mix cracker crumbs and butter until crumbly. Press mixture into the bottom of a greased 13"x9" baking pan; set aside. In a large bowl, combine remaining ingredients. Mix well and spread over crust. Bake at 350 degrees for 25 to 28 minutes, until edges are golden. Cool; cut into bars. Makes 2-1/2 dozen.

Christmas Eve at our grandparents' house was a special memory that lingers in my heart. All the aunts, uncles and cousins were there. I remember when I was a small girl there was always a wreath filled with nougat candies hanging on the door in Gramma's living room. Each person was only allowed to have one piece of candy so there was enough to go around. It was just a small treat but something we still cherish. My grandparents are both gone now, but at our family Christmas party each year I still hand out just one piece of this special candy to each person. Together we eat it and recall the days in the past and the love we shared.

– Tammy Andrus, Howard, PA

Kris Kringle Tops

Angela Dagenbach
Harrison, OH

My Gramma Jess made these cookies every year for Christmas. My seven brothers and sisters and I couldn't wait to get to the platter of Kris Kringle Tops! After she passed away, I found the recipe among her things. Now my children include these cookies in their Christmas gatherings too.

18-1/2 oz. pkg. devil's food
   cake mix
2 eggs, lightly beaten
1/2 c. oil

1 T. water
Optional: 2/3 c. chopped
   walnuts
Garnish: powdered sugar

In a large bowl, mix together dry cake mix, eggs, oil, water and walnuts, if using. If dough is too sticky, add a bit of flour. Form dough into walnut-size balls; roll in powdered sugar. Place cookies on well greased or parchment paper-lined baking sheets, 2 inches apart. Bake at 375 degrees for 8 to 10 minutes. Cool on wire racks. Makes 2 to 3 dozen.

Family fun...build a yummy gingerbread house and top it off with chocolate bar doors and shutters!

Grandma's
Christmas Cookies

Belgian Waffle Cookies

Holly Miller
Howard, OH

My mother made these cookies every Christmas for our family and for our schoolteachers. Now I make them for my own family. They're always a big hit!

6 c. all-purpose flour
2 c. sugar
2 c. brown sugar, packed
8 eggs, beaten

1 lb. butter, melted and slightly cooled
2 T. vanilla extract
Optional: powdered sugar

Combine all ingredients except optional powdered sugar in a large bowl. Mix well. Spray a waffle iron with non-stick vegetable spray. Place one tablespoon batter at a time onto preheated waffle iron. Cook until golden, according to manufacturer's instructions. Remove to a wire rack. Sprinkle with powdered sugar, if desired. Store in a covered container or plastic zipping bag. Cookies may be wrapped and frozen up to 2 weeks. Makes 4 to 5 dozen.

White Christmas Mocha

Erin Stamile
Waco, TX

I love to make this warm beverage whenever I go Christmas shopping with friends. Just pack a thermos and some disposable cups for portable Christmas cheer!

2 c. milk
1/2 c. white chocolate chips
2 peppermint candy canes, crushed and divided

2 T. instant coffee granules, or 1 c. strong brewed coffee
Garnish: whipped cream

Combine milk, chocolate chips and half of crushed candy over medium-low heat. Cook until chips and candy are melted; stir in coffee. Ladle into mugs. Top with whipped cream and remaining crushed candy. Makes about 4 servings.

Buttermilk Sugar Cookies

Pamelyn Hooley
Lagrange, IN

I've been making these cookies for Christmas since my children were little. Now my grandchildren like to frost and sprinkle too. So delicious and pretty...much faster than cut-out cookies!

1 c. shortening	4-1/2 c. all-purpose flour
1-1/2 c. sugar	1 t. baking soda
2 eggs, beaten	2 t. baking powder
1 c. buttermilk	1/4 t. salt
1 t. vanilla extract	Garnish: candy sprinkles

In a large bowl, blend together shortening and sugar. Stir in eggs, buttermilk and vanilla. Add remaining ingredients except garnish; mix well. Drop dough by 2 tablespoonfuls per cookie onto greased baking sheets. Press down cookies with the bottom of a buttered, sugared glass. Bake at 350 degrees for 9 to 13 minutes. Cool. Decorate with Cream Cheese Frosting and sprinkles. Makes 4 dozen.

Cream Cheese Frosting:

8-oz. pkg. cream cheese, softened	1 t. vanilla extract
1/2 c. butter, softened	16-oz. pkg. powdered sugar

Blend together cream cheese, butter and vanilla. Gradually stir in powdered sugar until smooth.

Here's a simple tip to help cut-out cookie shapes bake up neatly. Place cookies on a parchment paper-lined baking sheet and pop into the fridge for 10 to 15 minutes, then bake.

Peekaberry Boos

Clair Shearer
Greene, NY

These jam-filled treats were my husband's favorite cookie that his mom used to make for him as a child.

2-1/2 c. all-purpose flour	1/4 c. sugar
1 t. baking soda	2 eggs, beaten
1 t. salt	1/2 c. water
1/2 t. cinnamon	1 t. vanilla extract
1/2 c. butter	2 c. quick-cooking oats,
1/2 c. shortening	uncooked
1 c. brown sugar, packed	2/3 c. seedless raspberry jam

In a bowl, mix together flour, baking soda, salt and cinnamon; set aside. In a separate large bowl, blend together butter and shortening. Gradually add sugars; blend well. Add eggs, water and vanilla; beat well. Add flour mixture and oats alternately to butter mixture; stir well. Drop dough by rounded teaspoonfuls onto ungreased baking sheets. Place 1/2 teaspoon jam on each cookie, pressing jam lightly into dough. Top with a level teaspoonful of remaining dough. Bake at 400 degrees for 10 to 12 minutes. Makes 4 dozen.

When cookie baking is a family affair, dress little ones in washable clothes and aprons. Be sure to take lots of pictures!

Irish Lace Cookies

Laurie Rupsis
Aiken, SC

These cookies are very delicate but well worth baking! They do not freeze well, but are quick & easy to do the day you need them.

1/2 c. butter, softened
3/4 c. light brown sugar, packed
2 T. all-purpose flour
2 T. milk

1 t. vanilla extract
1-1/2 c. long-cooking oats,
    uncooked

In a large bowl, blend butter and brown sugar until fluffy. Beat in flour, milk and vanilla; stir in oats. Drop dough by rounded teaspoonfuls onto aluminum foil-lined baking sheets, no more than 12 per sheet. Bake at 350 degrees for 10 to 12 minutes, until golden. Allow cookies to cool on baking sheets for one minutes. Carefully remove to wire racks to cool completely. Makes 3 dozen.

Turn flea-market finds into charming one-of-a-kind cookie stands. Use china and glass cement to attach a porcelain or glass plate atop a candleholder or vase... so easy, you'll want to make some to share!

Chinese Chews

Cathy Nign
Temple City, CA

*My grandmother made these old-fashioned cookies every Christmas.
I don't know where the name came from, but the cookies are sweet,
cakelike, chewy and very easy to make.*

3/4 c. all-purpose flour
1 c. sugar
1/4 t. salt
1 t. baking powder

1 c. chopped dates
1 c. chopped walnuts
3 eggs, well beaten
Garnish: powdered sugar

In a bowl, mix together flour, sugar, baking powder and salt. Stir in dates and walnuts; add eggs and mix well. Press mixture into a greased 10"x10" baking pan. Bake at 350 degrees for 30 minutes. Cut into squares; cool completely. Roll gently in powdered sugar. Makes one to 1-1/4 dozen.

My grandmother is an amazing crocheter. She made Christmas stockings for everyone in our large family. The best part of Christmas morning was going over to my grandparents' house and seeing all of our stockings hanging up waiting for us. She used different yarn for each of us so we all knew exactly which one to look for. We wouldn't get to open them until after the big meal, but we all loved to see them hanging there. They were as important as the Christmas tree itself. Years later my grandmother taught me how to crochet. I have since moved away and have started my own family but I feel close to her every time I pick up a crochet hook. This year I am making Christmas stockings for my two small boys. I hope they share the same excitement I did so long ago.

–Megan Swink, High Point, NC

Gram's Christmas Walnut Cut-Outs

Michelle Brownawell
Trevorton, PA

My gram always baked these cookies early in December. Then she wrapped them up and hid them away in her attic until Christmas. She said that was the secret to why they tasted so good. I liked to dunk them into my mom's morning coffee. This is how my obsession with dunking cookies into coffee began!

1 c. butter, softened
1 c. sugar
2 eggs, beaten
1/4 c. milk
2 t. vanilla extract
1 t. walnut extract

4 c. all-purpose flour
2 t. baking powder
1/4 c. walnuts, ground
Garnish: walnut halves,
   colored sugar

Blend butter and sugar in a large bowl until well combined. Add eggs, milk and extracts; beat until fluffy and set aside. In a separate bowl, mix flour, baking powder and walnuts. Gradually add flour mixture to butter mixture; beat until blended. On a floured surface, roll out dough 1/4-inch thick. Cut out shapes with cookie cutters. Place on ungreased baking sheets; press a walnut half into the center of each. Bake at 350 degrees for 12 to 14 minutes, until golden; don't overbake. Remove to wire racks; cool completely. Frost with Coffee Icing; sprinkle with colored sugar. Makes 6 dozen.

Coffee Icing:

1/3 c. butter
3 c. powdered sugar
1-1/2 t. vanilla extract

1 t. maple extract
2 T. strong brewed coffee,
   cooled

Combine butter, powdered sugar and extracts. Stir in enough coffee to form a spreading consistency.

Wheeling Cookies

Sharon Vale
Irving, TX

These were some of my favorite cookies growing up. This recipe was handed down to me by my grandmother. I don't know why they're called Wheeling Cookies...perhaps because we lived in Martins Ferry, Ohio, right across the river from Wheeling, West Virginia. For Christmas I like to use red and green gumdrops. Assorted colors of gumdrops make pretty cookies for bridal showers.

3/4 c. shortening
3/4 c. sugar
2 eggs, beaten
1/2 t. vanilla extract
1/2 t. lemon extract

1-1/4 t. baking powder
2-1/4 c. all-purpose flour
11-oz. pkg. mini spicy
   gumdrops
Garnish: powdered sugar

In a large bowl, blend shortening and sugar; add eggs, one at a time. Add extracts, baking powder and flour; mix well. Form dough into walnut-size balls; place on ungreased baking sheets. Press one gumdrop on top of each cookie. Bake at 350 degrees for 12 to 14 minutes, until the bottoms are lightly golden. Remove cookies from baking sheets; immediately sprinkle with powdered sugar. Makes 4 dozen.

Use a mini ice cream scoop to drop cookie dough onto baking sheets, or roll dough into a log, chill and slice.

Dolce De Burro

Carmela Seagull
Amherstburg, Ontario

Christmas isn't Christmas without these Italian cookies on our table! This recipe has been in our family for generations. My dad always cracked the walnuts so they would be fresh, then my mom baked the cookies and we kids rolled them in the powdered sugar.

1 c. butter, softened
1-3/4 c. powdered sugar,
   divided

1 t. vanilla extract
2 c. all-purpose flour
1 c. walnuts, finely chopped

In a large bowl, combine butter, 3/4 cup powdered sugar and vanilla. Stir until creamy. Slowly stir in flour and walnuts. Form into 3/4-inch balls. Place cookies 1/2-inch apart on ungreased baking sheets. Bake at 300 degrees for 25 to 30 minutes, until cream colored. Remove cookies to wire racks. Cool until just warm to the touch; roll in remaining powdered sugar. Cool completely; roll again in the same powdered sugar. Store in a tightly covered container. Makes 3 dozen.

Poinsettia Punch

Hope Davenport
Portland, TX

My mom gave me this delicious holiday punch recipe. With its sweet holiday name and pretty color, we love to make it for December parties.

12-oz. can frozen pink
   lemonade concentrate,
   thawed

2 ltrs. ginger ale, chilled
1 qt. raspberry sherbet, softened

Combine lemonade and ginger ale in a punch bowl. Just before serving, add sherbet by heaping tablespoons; stir gently. Makes about 13 cups.

Give punch cups a sweet touch...dip the rims of
chilled glasses in water, then in sparkly sugar.

Grandma's
Christmas Cookies

Oh-So-Good Nuggets

Jenita Davison
La Plata, MO

Grandma started making these when our kids were little...they quickly became a favorite. I think she found the original recipe on the back of a cereal box. It's even great to grab a bag for a carry-along breakfast on shopping days.

6 c. doughnut-shaped oat cereal
   and/or bite-size crispy rice or
   corn cereal squares
1 c. sweetened dried cranberries,
   raisins or chopped dates
1 c. salted peanuts or pecans,
   chopped

1/2 c. butter, sliced
1/4 c. light corn syrup
1 c. light brown sugar, packed
1/2 t. salt
1/2 t. baking soda

Combine cereal, fruit and nuts in a large heat-proof bowl; set aside. In a large saucepan over medium heat, combine butter, corn syrup, brown sugar and salt. Cook until mixture starts bubbling. Continue cooking, uncovered, for 2 minutes. Remove from heat; stir in baking soda. Pour over cereal mixture; stir to coat well. Spread mixture in 2 greased 13"x9" baking pans. Bake at 250 degrees for 15 minutes. Let cool 10 minutes. Break into bite-size pieces, as needed. Store in an airtight container. Makes 12 servings.

Whip up some super-simple ornaments. Trace a cookie cutter onto doubled felt and cut out, then blanket-stitch together and stuff lightly...so cute!

Suzy's Snowballs

Suzy Mechling
Round Rock, TX

After high school, I went to a floral and design school in Boston, Massachusetts. Two classmates and I weren't able to go home for the holidays, so our House Director took us to her home. We made Christmas cookies together and these were one of my favorites.

1 c. butter, sliced
1 c. sugar
1 c. chopped dates
1 egg, beaten
1/2 t. vanilla extract

2 c. crispy rice cereal
1/2 c. chopped pecans
2 7-oz. pkgs. sweetened flaked
   coconut

Melt butter in a large saucepan over medium-low heat. Add sugar, dates and egg. Cook, stirring constantly, for 10 minutes. Cool slightly. Add vanilla, cereal and pecans; mix well. Form into balls, 2 teaspoons dough per ball; roll in coconut spread on wax paper. Place balls on a plate or baking sheet. Cover and refrigerate for several hours, until set. Store in an airtight container. Makes 3 dozen.

Sugar Cookie Dough

Super-speedy snickerdoodle cookies! Roll a tube of refrigerated sugar cookie dough into one-inch balls. Coat them in a mixture of 3 tablespoons sugar and one teaspoon cinnamon. Bake on ungreased baking sheets, 10 to 13 minutes at 350 degrees.

Swedish Horns

Liz Cesal
Tampa, FL

I make these crescent-shaped cookies every Christmas and our family really loves them. The recipe was handed down from my grandmother to my mother, then to me.

1 lb. butter, room temperature
4 c. all-purpose flour
4 egg yolks, beaten, room
   temperature
16-oz. container sour cream,
   room temperature

1/2 to 1 c. powdered sugar
12-oz. jar peach or apricot
   preserves
Garnish: additional powdered
   sugar

In a large bowl, blend butter with flour, using your hands. Mix in egg yolks and sour cream; dough will be sticky. Form dough into 15 balls, each 2 inches in diameter. Place balls in a bowl; cover and refrigerate overnight. Lightly sprinkle powdered sugar over the work surface. Roll out balls, one at a time, into 6-inch circles; cut each circle into 5 triangles. Spoon 1/2 teaspoon preserves onto each triangle. Roll up, starting at the wide end; tuck in ends and curve into a half-moon shape. Place cookies on greased baking sheets. Bake at 350 degrees for 30 to 35 minutes. Cool; sprinkle with powdered sugar. Makes about 6 dozen.

Cheery holiday potholders with pockets can be found at any grocery. Slip several wrapped cookies (and the recipe!) into the pocket for handy keep-on-hand gifts.

Spicy Ginger Crinkles

Rachel Harter
The Woodlands, TX

My grandmother and mother taught me to bake cookies when I was a young girl. This simple one-bowl recipe is one we created together. It's sweet and spicy...perfect with apple cider or hot cocoa. I am newly married, and my husband and I shared our first Christmas together last year. These cookies were the first ones I made to celebrate the season.

2/3 c. canola oil
1 c. sugar
1 egg, beaten
1/4 c. molasses
2 c. all-purpose flour

1 t. baking soda
1/2 t. salt
1 t. cinnamon
1 t. ground ginger
Garnish: additional sugar

Combine all ingredients except garnish in a large bowl. Stir well to combine. Form dough into one-inch balls. Roll each ball in sugar; place on greased baking sheets. With a fork, lightly press the top of each ball twice to make a lattice design. Bake at 350 degrees for 12 to 15 minutes; cool. Makes about 3 dozen.

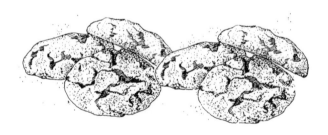

Light molasses has a sweet, mild taste best for waffles and pancakes. For baking, dark molasses, which is less sweet and thicker, is best. In a pinch, they can be interchanged, but to get that robust molasses flavor in a cookie, dark molasses is the best choice.

Jam Tarts

Carolyn Jollimore
Hubbards, Nova Scotia

This is an old recipe that my mom made all the time when my brother, sister and I were growing up, especially at Christmas. They are our favorite cookies. Since then they have become my hubby's favorite cookies too.

3/4 c. butter, softened
3/4 c. light brown sugar, packed
1 egg, well beaten
1 T. milk or fruit juice
1 t. vanilla extract

1-1/2 c. all-purpose flour
1/2 t. baking powder
1/4 t. salt
1/2 c. favorite fruit jam or jelly

In a large bowl, beat butter and brown sugar until creamy. Beat in egg, milk or juice and vanilla; set aside. In a separate bowl, combine flour, baking powder and salt. Add flour mixture to butter mixture; beat until smoothly combined. Place 2 teaspoons dough into each of 24 greased mini muffin cups. Make an indentation in each with a floured finger. Spoon one teaspoon jam or jelly into each cup. Bake at 375 degrees for 15 to 20 minutes. until slightly puffy and lightly golden. Cool slightly before removing from tins. Makes 2 dozen.

Old-fashioned fun! Keep kids busy making salt dough ornaments. Mix 2 cups flour, one cup salt and one cup water. Knead well; roll out dough 1/2-inch thick. Cut into shapes with cookie cutters and punch a hole for a hanger. Bake at 200 degrees for 15 minutes, or until hardened. Paint with craft paints.

Banana Spice Cookies

Celeste Peck
Griswold, IA

I could hardly contain myself on Christmas Eve day, knowing Grandma would soon be coming with the big white box. Inside were wonderful freshly baked cookies, tinted pink, yellow, green and even light blue. After I'd whined a little, Grams would let me have one cookie...just one! More would be permitted after supper. I will never forget looking out the window and seeing Grams walking to our house with the box. The best part was raising the lid and seeing all the layers of cookies carefully tucked between layers of wax paper.

1/2 c. shortening
1 c. brown sugar, packed
2 eggs, beaten
1 c. ripe bananas, mashed
2 c. all-purpose flour
2 t. baking powder

1/4 t. baking soda
1/4 t. salt
1/4 t. ground cloves
1/2 t. cinnamon
1/2 c. chopped pecans
Optional: pecan halves

In a large bowl, blend shortening, sugar and eggs; stir in bananas and set aside. Sift flour into a separate bowl. Add baking powder, baking soda, salt and spices; sift again. Stir flour mixture into shortening mixture; stir in nuts. Cover and chill one hour. Drop dough by rounded tablespoonfuls onto lightly greased baking sheets, 2 inches apart. Bake at 375 degrees for 8 to 10 minutes. Cool. Frost cookies with Confectioner's Icing. Top each with a pecan half, if desired. Makes 3 dozen.

Confectioner's Icing:

1 c. powdered sugar
1-1/2 T. light cream or whole
   milk

1/2 t. vanilla extract
Optional: few drops food
   coloring

Combine powdered sugar, cream or milk and vanilla. Stir until smooth, adding a little more cream or milk if necessary. Tint with food coloring, if desired.

Be a cookie elf! Wrap up plates of cookies to leave secretly
at the neighbors' doorsteps...and don't get caught!

Holly Wreath Cookies

Maggie Ham
Brandywine, MD

My grandmother used to send us a tin of cookies each Christmas. These were the ones that my younger brother and I most looked forward to. They are even tastier now that they bring back those memories, since she is no longer with us.

1 c. butter, softened	1/2 t. salt
1/2 c. powdered sugar	1-1/2 c. long-cooking oats,
2 t. vanilla extract	uncooked
2 c. all-purpose flour	

In a large bowl, beat butter until creamy. Add sugar gradually, beating until fluffy. Stir in vanilla and set aside. In a separate bowl, sift flour and salt together. Add flour mixture to butter mixture; stir thoroughly. Stir in oats, working with hands if necessary. Dough will be very stiff. Roll out on a lightly floured surface, 1/8-inch thick. Cut out with a round cookie cutter; place cookies on ungreased baking sheets. Bake at 325 degrees for 15 minutes. Decorate cookies with Thin Frosting. Makes about 3 dozen.

Thin Frosting:

2 c. powdered sugar	1 t. vanilla extract
3 T. fruit juice or water	

Combine all ingredients; stir until thin and smooth.

Wrap up some home-baked treats to send to a service person overseas...they're sure to be appreciated. Tuck in a note that says, "We're thinking of you." The American Red Cross can tell you how to mail your care packages.

Bedtime Cookies

Carol Craver
Oakland, MD

My Grandma Mary kept her ten children fed and often fed the farmhands too. Everything was so delicious! She made these cookies by the crock-full for her 28 grandchildren.

1 c. butter, softened
1/2 c. shortening
1 c. sugar
1 c. brown sugar, packed
3 eggs, lightly beaten
1 t. vanilla extract

Optional: 1/2 t. black walnut
  extract
4-1/2 c. all-purpose flour
2 t. baking soda
1 t. salt
1 c. black walnuts, chopped

In a large bowl, blend butter, shortening and sugars. Add eggs and extracts; beat very well and set aside. In a separate bowl, sift together flour, baking soda and salt. Add flour mixture to sugar mixture; mix well and stir in nuts. Dough will be stiff. Divide dough into 2 equal parts. Form each part into a roll, 8 to 10 inches long and 2 inches thick. Wrap rolls in plastic wrap; refrigerate overnight. Slice dough 1/4-inch thick; place on parchment paper-lined baking sheets. Bake at 350 degrees for 10 to 12 minutes, until very lightly golden. Makes 4 dozen.

Best of all are the decorations the grandchildren have made... fat little stars and rather crooked Santas, shaped out of dough and baked in the oven.

–Gladys Taber

Grandma's
Christmas Cookies

Emma's Casserole Cookies

Peggy Donnally
Toledo, OH

This recipe was handed down from my mother-in-law. She made tin upon tin of the most delicious Christmas cookies, which she stored on her summer porch. I got very good at memorizing which cookies were kept in which decorated tin for those stealthy cookie raids. These are a particular favorite of mine...they're decadently rich and a quick, no-fuss addition to any holiday cookie tray.

2 eggs, beaten
1 c. sugar
1 c. chopped dates
1 c. sweetened flaked coconut

1 c. chopped walnuts
1 t. vanilla extract
1/4 t. almond extract
Garnish: powdered sugar

In a large bowl, mix eggs and sugar until light and fluffy. Stir in remaining ingredients except garnish. Transfer mixture to a 2-quart casserole dish coated with non-stick vegetable spray. Bake at 350 degrees for 30 minutes. Remove from oven; stir well with a wooden spoon. Cool; roll into 3/4-inch balls. Roll balls in powdered sugar. Makes 3 dozen.

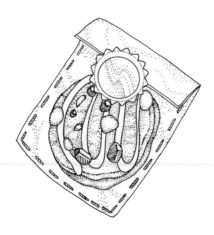

A terrific party favor...jumbo cookies tucked into paper CD envelopes from the office supply store. Decorate the envelopes with stickers or rubber stamps. Your guests will thank you!

Grandma's Chocolate Bon-Bons

Susan Jacobs
Vista, CA

My husband's grandmother gave me a recipe booklet compiled by the Jefferson Volunteer Fire Company Ladies Auxiliary in 1974. In the booklet was Grandma's own recipe for these chocolate bon-bons. For the next 20 years or so, I made these for Christmas, giving them as gifts and serving at family gatherings. Recently everyone misses them, so I thought I'd make them again this year. These are a great gift or cookie swap treat.

1 c. graham cracker crumbs
16-oz. pkg. powdered sugar
1 c. sweetened flaked coconut
1 c. margarine, softened

1-1/2 c. creamy peanut butter
12-oz. pkg. semi-sweet
   chocolate chips
2 T. shortening

In a large bowl, combine cracker crumbs, powdered sugar and coconut. Add margarine and peanut butter; mix well. Roll mixture into walnut-size balls. Place balls on wax paper; refrigerate until ready to dip in chocolate. Melt chocolate chips with shortening in the top of a double boiler over hot water. Stir until chocolate is melted and smooth. With a fork, dip bon-bons into chocolate, one at a time, coating well. Remove bon-bons to a sheet of wax paper. Return to refrigerator until firm. Makes 4 dozen.

Homemade candy is always a welcome gift! Make the gift even sweeter...place individual candies in mini paper muffin cups and arrange in a decorated box.

Grandma's Christmas Cookies

Grandma Franz's Popcorn Balls

Katie Majeske
Denver, PA

This is one of the handwritten recipes I have from my grandmother. It is dated 1965. I remember going to her home at Christmas and finding a large speckled melamine bowl full of these popcorn balls. She would add a little red and green food coloring to the mixture for the holiday. They are so yummy!

20 c. popped popcorn
Optional: 2 c. peanuts
1/2 c. butter, sliced

10-oz. pkg. marshmallows
Optional: few drops food
   coloring

Place popped popcorn in a large roaster pan or heat-proof bowl. Mix in peanuts, if using; set aside. In a saucepan over medium-low heat, melt butter and marshmallows. Stir in food coloring, if desired; pour over popcorn. Let cool a few minutes. With buttered hands, form into 3-inch balls. Makes one to 1-1/4 dozen.

I grew up on a dairy farm where we spent hours every late afternoon to early evening out in the barn caring for the calves and milking the cows. I remember during the couple weeks before Christmas, on many nights we would return to the house to find that my mom had made special Christmas cookies or candy. The sweet aroma filled the house when we walked in. What a treat to enjoy after completing the chores on those cold winter nights before Christmas!

–Pamela Miller, Xenia, OH

Old-Fashioned Hard Tack Candy

Sheri Dulaney
Englewood, OH

I love making this candy, as the colors and flavors can be changed to fit any season or occasion. It's great to give as a gift, or just to keep sitting out in a pretty bowl for visitors!

2 c. sugar
1 c. water
1/4 c. light corn syrup

1/2 t. desired flavoring oil
1/2 to 1 t. food coloring to
   match flavoring

Line a 13"x9" baking pan with aluminum foil; set aside. In a saucepan over medium heat, combine sugar, water and corn syrup. Bring to a boil, stirring constantly, until sugar dissolves and mixture begins to boil. Cook without stirring until mixture reaches the hard-crack stage, or 290 to 310 degrees on a candy thermometer. Remove from heat. Quickly stir in flavoring oil and food coloring. Pour the hot syrup into the lined pan in a thin, even layer. When lukewarm, deeply score the slab of candy with a table knife into squares or triangles, as desired. When cold, carefully break pieces along the score lines. Wrap each piece individually with wax paper. Store at room temperature. Makes one pound.

Hard Tack Candy in glowing colors is so pretty...give it in a clear glass apothecary jar topped off with a bow.

Famous Chocolate Candy

Judy Scherer
Benton, MO

A friend gave us this recipe and we have made it the last couple of years at Christmas. It's easy to make.

1 lb. white melting chocolate,
   broken up
6-oz. pkg milk chocolate chips

1/2 c. creamy peanut butter
2-1/2 c. salted peanuts

Combine chocolates in a microwave-safe bowl. Microwave on high for one minute and 45 seconds; mix well. Add peanut butter; mix well. Stir in peanuts. Drop mixture by teaspoonfuls onto wax paper-lined baking sheets. Refrigerate until set. Store, loosely covered. Makes 30 to 40 pieces.

Mee-Mee's Butterscotch Fudge

Deborah Thompson
Taswell, IN

My grandmother made this fudge every Christmas. She has been gone since 1980, so making it at Christmas gives me a little of her love for the holidays that she enjoyed so much!

2 6-oz. pkgs. butterscotch chips
1/2 c. crunchy peanut butter

2/3 c. sweetened condensed
   milk

Grease a 9"x9" baking pan or line with aluminum foil; set aside. In the top of a double boiler, combine butterscotch chips and peanut butter. Stir over hot (not boiling) water until butterscotch chips melt; stir until blended. Add condensed milk; stir just until blended. Spread mixture in pan; chill until firm. Cut into squares. Makes 1-1/2 pounds.

Index

Index

Index

Find Gooseberry Patch
wherever you are!

www.gooseberrypatch.com

Call us toll-free at 1·800·854·6673

handknit mittens

strings of popcorn

homemade candy

letters to Santa

paper snowflakes

curling ribbons

sugar cookies

holly & mistletoe

U.S. to Metric Recipe Equivalents

Volume Measurements

1/4 teaspoon	1 mL
1/2 teaspoon	2 mL
1 teaspoon	5 mL
1 tablespoon = 3 teaspoons	15 mL
2 tablespoons = 1 fluid ounce	30 mL
1/4 cup	60 mL
1/3 cup	75 mL
1/2 cup = 4 fluid ounces	125 mL
1 cup = 8 fluid ounces	250 mL
2 cups = 1 pint =16 fluid ounces	500 mL
4 cups = 1 quart	1 L

Weights

1 ounce	30 g
4 ounces	120 g
8 ounces	225 g
16 ounces = 1 pound	450 g

Oven Temperatures

300° F	150° C
325° F	160° C
350° F	180° C
375° F	190° C
400° F	200° C
450° F	230° C

Baking Pan Sizes

Square

8x8x2 inches	2 L = 20x20x5 cm
9x9x2 inches	2.5 L = 23x23x5 cm

Rectangular

13x9x2 inches	3.5 L = 33x23x5 cm

Loaf

9x5x3 inches	2 L = 23x13x7 cm

Round

8x1-1/2 inches	1.2 L = 20x4 cm
9x1-1/2 inches	1.5 L = 23x4 cm